Royal Australian Regiment. Kapyong.

"And everybody praised the Duke,
Who this great fight did win."
"But what good came of it at last?"
Quoth little Peterkin.
"Why, that I cannot tell,"said he.
"But 'twas a famous victory."

Robert Southey, The Battle of Blenheim.

THE MILITARY PAINTINGS OF TERENCE CUNEO

BRIGADIER GERALD LANDY

New Cavendish Books

ACKNOWLEDGEMENTS

Terence Cuneo, Gerald Landy and the publishers are deeply grateful to all the corps, regiments, organisations and individuals who have contributed to the production of this book. Some have provided colour transparencies of pictures in their possession, others have given historical background information and still others have passed on anecdotes, or allowed their own published words to be quoted, to enhance and enliven the captions. It would have been impossible to complete this anthology of Cuneo's military art without their active assistance. This generous help, always so readily given, is most warmly acknowledged.

First edition published in Great Britain by New Cavendish Books – 1993

Design and typesetting – John B Cooper
Production and supervision – Narisa Chakra
Editorial direction – Allen Levy

Printed and bound in Hong Kong under the supervision of Mandarin Offset, London.
New Cavendish Books, 3 Denbigh Road, London W11 2SJ

ISBN 1 872727 51 4

Contents

Terence Cuneo with Challenger tank at Bovington.(Photograph courtesy of Geoff Wilkinson)

Foreword

General Sir Martin Farndale, KCB
Master Gunner, St James's Park

No artist has done more to record the achievements of the British Armed Forces, especially the Army, than Terence Cuneo. He has devoted a lifetime to this task. Although his efforts in the fields of railways and industry, portraiture and landscape have been much acclaimed, it is likely that his military paintings will prove to be the work for which he will be best remembered.

This book is a unique collection and as one turns the pages great national events, stirring moments in battle and fascinating glimpses of military ceremonial are revealed. From Cuneo's paintings future generations will learn much about great occasions of the past, even those which were photographed – for no photograph can capture the understanding, compassion and insight with which Cuneo invests his work.

I know him well and have been put to the test by him many times as he asked "What exact time of day do you wish me to record?", or "What exact moment in the battle am I to portray ?". Such questions have caused much research and wonder. His insistence on recreating events with men and equipment in order to get every detail exactly right, not so much to show how it is meant to be done but rather how men actually do it when under stress, has caused much critical self-examination in the Army. His eye for detail and authenticity as he directs the reconstruction of part of 'Killiecrankie', 'Sidi Rezegh', 'Kohima', 'Hyderabad' or some ceremonial event is as penetrating as that of the most exacting drill sergeant. I have seen him perched high in a chemist's shop to record a 'freedom' parade in Nottingham, or leaning precariously from a helicopter to record the last great 'battle' of the Cold War – Exercise Lionheart. Others will have had similar experiences. I once watched him move 21st Panzer Division with a few strokes of his brush when those who had been there said that what he had done was not quite right! But I have never heard his finished work criticised for inaccuracy.

Somehow an Army like ours needs great ceremonial parades to keep it up to the mark for war, to sustain its pride, morale, confidence and ability to organise to perfection. Cuneo can portray all this in a way that few, if any, can match. When he turns to battle scenes he manages to convey the sheer horror, stupidity and waste of war; look at the scenes of Kohima, 5th Battery under gas attack in World War I and some of his paintings of the Gulf War. Perhaps the day will come when mankind learns to live without war and then future generations will look with incredulity as they see from his paintings what man has done to man – and to animals – over the centuries. Perhaps if we are constantly reminded of this we may be able to ensure that it never occurs again and remember how vital it is to have strong defences. The maintenance of peace and security must be the greatest of all man's endeavours; without this we have nothing at all.

Because he devotes his full energy to his work, because he understands how men live and labour, Cuneo is respected and loved by all who have had the privilege of working with him. Indeed, Terence Cuneo is recognised as **the** artist of the British Army of the 20th century and I know that I act for many when I salute, thank and congratulate him for all that he has done.

Woolwich
1 November 1993

The Military Paintings of Terence Cuneo

The boy thought it was the nicest present he'd ever had. The shiny black tin contained ten small tablets of different colours which, when he mixed them with water, produced hues of seemingly endless variety. He looked at the pencil sketch he had been working on. How drab it seemed. But now he could bring it to life. Quickly he began to mix some of the colours, applying them boldly to his drawing. At first they ran into each other a bit but he soon got the hang of how much water to use and gave never a thought to what his mother might say when she saw the cuffs of his white shirt. For several minutes he worked steadily, deep in concentration. The tip of his tongue protruded from the corner of his mouth as he leant closer to the desk to fill in a detail of the soldier's uniform. Burnt sienna had been perfect for the khaki and perhaps, with a little more water, it would do for the face as well. But then, he thought, a touch of rose madder would give a fresher complexion, and it was a colour he had always liked. Satisfied, he moved on to complete the soldier's helmet and moustache and paused to survey the total effect. Excellent! Soldier number 5 was finished, identical in height and every detail of uniform with soldiers 1, 2, 3 and 4 and, like his comrades, with jet black moustache and eyes of cobalt blue. Only three more to be coloured in and the detachment would be complete. If he kept going he could finish the picture before bedtime. What should he call it? 'Off to War'?, 'Into Battle'?, 'For King and Country'? Faintly, he heard his mother's voice, "Have you finished your homework, dear? Supper is almost ready." Why, he wondered, was his mother always so concerned about things like homework and food, especially when he was busy on his first military picture. He resolved to get up very early in the morning and finish the work before the household became preoccupied with

Childhood sketches.

baths, breakfast, laundry and the countless other aspects of the daily round by which his mother set such store but which, apart from breakfast, he regarded with indifference.

The year was 1915. The boy was seven. His name was Terence Cuneo. In the years that lay ahead he would learn about form, perspective and the use of colour from his parents, who were both artists, from teachers at art school and from experience. He would go on to become a painter of renown but he would never lose the lively enthusiasm, directness and sense of urgency he showed as a child. Painting is at once Cuneo's work and his relaxation. He is a prolific artist and during a professional career of more than 60 years has portrayed with insight and power a wide range of human endeavour. Whatever his final place in the history of art of the 20th century – and he has painted his way through most of it – it is unlikely that any other contemporary British artist will be found to have made a more comprehensive or more popularly accepted contribution to the record of our time.

In 1977 Terence Cuneo wrote his autobiography *The Mouse and His Master*. It was a reflective and remarkably objective appraisal of his own work, presenting some 300 examples of his drawings and paintings – landscapes, portraits, state occasions of pomp and circumstance, scenes of battle, equestrian studies in great variety, sombre selections from his years as a war artist, many of his enchanting 'mousterpieces' and a marshalling-yard's-worth of railway engines of almost every known class.

It is probably as a railway painter that Cuneo is best known and his work is celebrated in the book *Terence Cuneo – Railway Painter of the Century*. He has always loved everything about railways, especially the great locomotives. Some of his earliest work in oils was commissioned by the major companies of the steam age with the aim of encouraging holiday-makers to travel by rail. The resultant colour posters were not only brilliantly successful in their commercial objective but are now recognised as classic examples of the genre. The quality of this work was exceptional and in one respect – its standard of technical accuracy – virtually unique.

Terence Cuneo's talent is, in part, hereditary. He was born on 1 November 1907, the only son of Cyrus Cincinnati Cuneo and Nell Tenison. His father, born in the United States, was of Italian extraction. Anna, his paternal grandmother, was a descendant of the great Italian patriot and soldier Giuseppe Garibaldi. His mother, Nell, was a cousin of the Victorian Poet Laureate, Alfred Lord Tennyson. It would be hard to imagine a more romantic and auspicious background for the arrival of the young Cuneo, but he was obliged to wait for some weeks after his birth before being given a first name. Cyrus and Nell, feeling perhaps that the surname was distinction enough, or that the child would surely find the level of fame that makes first names superfluous, were in no mood to be hurried into observing conventions. The choice of name was made in unusual circumstances. The new parents were keen theatre-goers and went one night to see a play in which an actor Terence de Marney was appearing. For reasons known only to himself, Cuneo senior was greatly taken with 'Terence'. Whatever the reasons they were enough to make Cyrus decide to give his infant a name for which, to this day, the son has no special liking.

The meeting of Cyrus and Nell, in Paris, was the stuff of romantic fiction. For two years Cyrus had been living in a garret in the Latin Quarter scraping along on a near-starvation diet and making some small income from giving boxing lessons to pay for his studies and the rent (Cyrus had been a flyweight Champion of San Francisco). One day a determined young Englishwoman arrived at the Gare de Lyon on her way to pursue, against parental advice, her studies at the Carlo Rossi Academy of Art, where Whistler gave instruction. His head student was Cyrus. The young woman was Nell. It was love at first sight. Two years later she persuaded Ciro, as she called him, to move to London to exploit his artistic talent. They were married in England in 1903.

Cuneo's recollections of his early childhood are of loving parents who, on the whole, managed to fit him into their busy schedule quite well, although they relied on a succession of nurses to attend to his material needs. The real warmth of his father's affection can be seen in a portrait of the baby Terence being nursed in bed by his mother. It is a picture of great charm, light and delicacy, which could have been painted only by an artist deeply in love with his two sitters.

Tragically, Cyrus Cuneo was to die of blood-poisoning at the peak of his career when he was only 37 years old and his son three months short of his ninth birthday. Nevertheless, Cyrus had had a strong influence on the boy in many ways. Recognising his son's natural ability, he fanned every spark of artistic talent. There were also other, more violent, skills to be acquired. Cyrus knew the importance of

This painting, auctioned in 1915, raised enough money to buy two ambulances that were shipped out to France in the same year. Each bore the inscription 'The Cyrus Cuneo Ambulance'.

The Cyrus Cuneo Ambulance

This picture takes Cuneo back to his very young days: "Maybe it wasn't really as big as I thought, but to a child of seven the picture upon my father's easel looked enormous. The sight of this close-up, ring-side view of a professional fight invariably filled me with a sense of awe. It seemed to exude a disturbing reality; to give out the threatening odour of sweat, resin and embrocation that means 'the ring'. It reminded me, only too vividly, of my own association with the boxing glove. Father insisted that his son should be able to defend himself and, in the happy belief that it was good for me, gave me regular boxing lessons. I have no recollection of enjoying these excursions into the noble art of fisticuffs. Father's idea of a gentle tap sometimes had me reeling and dabbing at a bloody nose. The session always ended with him pretending to walk into a devastating left hook that sent him crashing to the ground. Whereupon my mother, whose anxiety was only partly feigned, would step forward, raise my hand in the air and pronounce me the winner by a knock-out."

physical fitness and encouraged his son to be active in sport. Thus Terence learned from his father the self-confidence that comes from nimble footwork and a good right cross.

If Terence was numbed by his father's death Nell was completely shattered. Her whole life had been devoted to helping Cyrus in his career and with her encouragement he had developed as an artist of considerable standing and an illustrator whose work was in constant demand by the best magazines in London. Nevertheless, her concern about Terence's future kept her going.

After schooling in Teignmouth and later, at Sutton Valence in Kent, Cuneo commenced his formal training in art at the Chelsea Polytechnic. He was 18 and bubbling with enthusiasm, but if he expected his artistic genius to be instantly recognised and acclaimed, he was to be disappointed. However, he was not downhearted and although he never established a cordial rapport with the Faculty his time at Chelsea was thoroughly enjoyable.

Many years were to pass before Cuneo began to establish his reputation as a military painter. But although the outstanding railway subjects came first, his military pictures match them in quality and are greater in number. They are not so widely known since few of them are accessible to the general public. Most are owned by the regiments and corps who commissioned them, notably the Royal Artillery and the Royal Engineers, and only rarely are these treasured possessions allowed to leave their hands. Happily, a number were made available for the 80th Birthday Retrospective of Cuneo's works in the Mall Galleries in London, opened by the Duke of Edinburgh on 10 June 1988 which was also Prince Philip's birthday. The appearance of these 'military' paintings whetted the appetite of the thousands who came to the show and Cuneo was pressed to make a larger selection available to a wider audience.

Cuneo's interest in painting military pictures began early. Like most small boys he was attracted by the uniform and manner of soldiers. They seemed colourful, vigorous and

'Midst shot and shell we made the narrow beach.'
Landing at Gallipoli, book illustration by Cyrus Cuneo.

noisy – everything about them suggested excitement and adventure. He had thrilled to stories of campaigns in India and Africa, of cavalry charges and Gordon of Khartoum, of fighting to defend the Empire, which at that time seemed to cover most of the World. Some specimens of his primitive military art, in which soldiers are seen to be uniform in height as well as in dress, are still in his possession.

Cuneo's respect and affection for the Army are strong and abiding. For his part, he has about him an air that strikes a chord with soldiers. He is a man's man, physically tough, forthright in manner, considerate and generous-hearted.

Mouse Drummer.

Highly professional in his attitude to work, he is at the same time debonair and amusing.

Early in his commercial career Cuneo came to be recognised as an outstanding 'action' illustrator. A shrewd editor sensed that he might also have the ability to spin a yarn in a way that would appeal to a youngster's yearning for adventure. Cuneo needed only one chance to show that as well as capturing with crayon the excitement of a cops and robbers chase, he could match that excitement with words that fired the imagination and his work was soon in great demand for boys' annuals and magazines.

Cuneo in his eighties has kept his enormous capacity for fun. No matter how important, solemn or official an occasion may be, his sense of mischief bubbles continuously and, especially on grand occasions, it is only a matter of a moment before it gets the better of him and he makes everyone laugh and relax. He can also be absurdly funny in private. An example comes to mind. Cuneo is in his studio with a sprightly friend – another octogenarian. The telephone rings. His friend answers, but it is a wrong number. Politely, his friend tells the caller, "I'm sorry but there's no Aunt Lucy here." In a twinkling Cuneo grasps the phone and, in a querulous falsetto, sobs "This is Aunt Lucy – I'm being held here against my will". A gust of boyish laughter blows the years away.

Hiding a mouse in his pictures is another of his jokes. The mouse has come to be regarded as a hall-mark of authenticity for his paintings, but it is much more than that and has a special purpose in his more sombre works. It is Cuneo's way of saying that it's all right to smile, even in the gravest situation – a philosophy to which soldiers, especially, readily respond. In a curious way the mouse, this "cow'rin, tim'rous beastie" has acquired a major role in Cuneo's work. At the unveiling of a new picture it is almost the first thing people look for. Naturally they express admiration for the artist's latest production but all the while their eyes sweep the canvas until eventually they are forced to ask the question –

The rout of the Afrika Korps. *Illustrated London News.*

The Sinking of 'The Simon Boilvior'. This painting had to be completed in a day and a night. *War Illustrated.*

"Where's the mouse?" There are certain rules to the game of 'hide-the-mouse'. The position, stance and, sometimes, the dress of the mouse must be relevant to the theme of the work and it must make a positive contribution. In a picture of say, Trooping the Colour, the mouse might be wearing the uniform of the particular regiment whose colour is being trooped and might be seen lowering his own small, but heraldically correct standard in the march-past. In scenes of battle he may be found with fixed bayonet. Occasionally he is allowed to take centre stage and appear in full regimental fig in his own right. A never-to-be-forgotten picture is that of the gallant Sir Thomas Blue-Vinney OGM (Order of the Golden Mousetrap) leading his troops in the Charge at Catnip Valley.

The years leading up to the outbreak of World War II were eventful for Terence Cuneo. In 1934 he had the great good fortune to marry Catherine (Cate) Munro who was to bring him much happiness, encouragement in his work and two daughters. It was Cate who gave him the support he needed to break out of a monotonous routine of magazine illustrations and seek more exciting challenges. It was a brave decision for a young couple with a family to support and inevitably led to a temporary reduction in earnings. But he was soon drawing regularly for 'quality' journals like *Good Housekeeping* and *Nash's Magazine*. Late in 1936 he began to work seriously in oils – a medium he took to at once as it well-suited his direct and vigorous style. From then on a large part of his published work was the reproduction of his oil paintings and he found himself in regular demand. However, these were the years of Hitler and the Nazis and, at the time of the Munich crisis in September 1938, Cuneo set off with two friends to join the Officers' Emergency Reserve. His friends were accepted, but he was turned down because of his father's nationality. Cuneo was incensed. He was a Londoner, born and bred, he couldn't even speak Italian and his father had been dead for over twenty years. It took him a long time to get over the bitter sense of rejection that this episode created but in due course he joined the LDV (Local Defence

An RAF Hurricane flying low to strafe French munitions trains.

Wartime magazine cover illustration.

The front cover and spreads from *'Tanks and how to draw them'*.

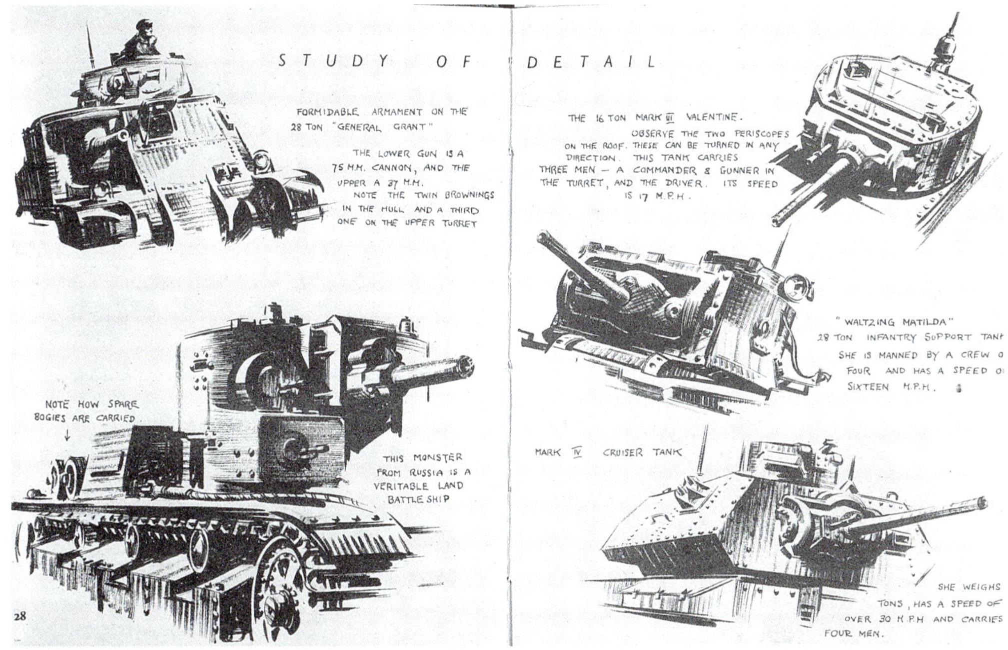

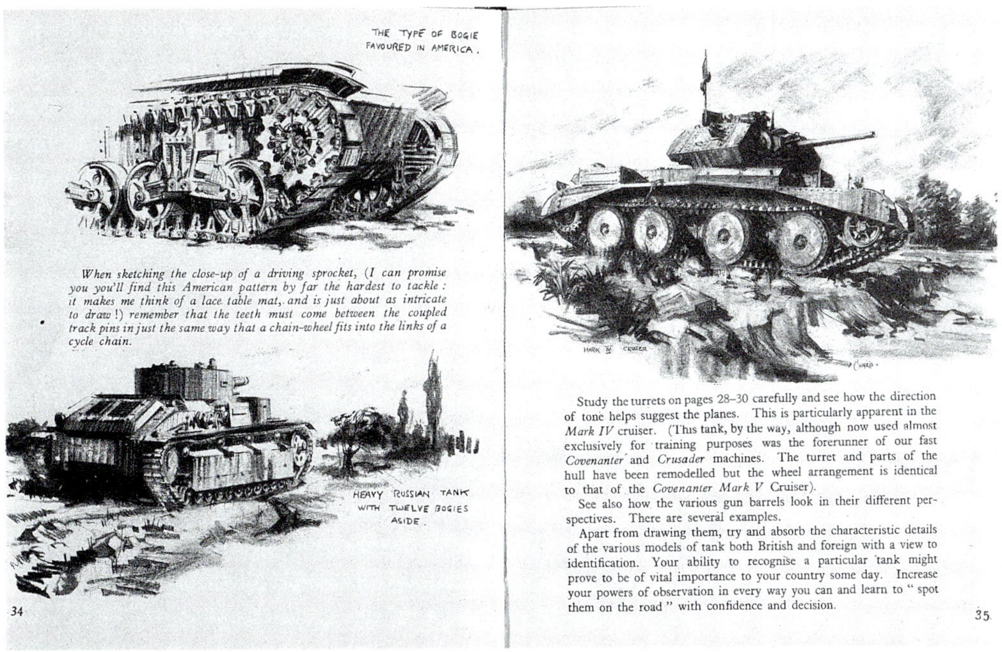

A selection of drawings from 'The Unconquerable Soul' exhibition.

Volunteers) which later became the Home Guard (Dad's Army).

When the war broke out on 3 September 1939, many of the magazines he worked for closed down, but simultaneously a new demand arose for war illustrations for such periodicals as *War Illustrated*, *Illustrated London News* and *Picture Post*. In the spring of 1940 he was asked by Sir Bruce Ingram, editor of ILN, to join a party of journalists, as the only artist, to report on the French war effort, in particular the conditions in their factories. The trip turned out to be more exciting than any of them had bargained for. While they were there, the Germans invaded France and Cuneo and his friends made their escape from Le Havre by the skin of their teeth.

Towards the end of 1941 Cuneo received an official request to go to Osset in Yorkshire to join the Royal Corps of Signals. There began a period which he regards as the most frustrating of his life. To put it mildly he and his new Corps were incompatible and he could never get to grips with even the most elementary aspect of Signals work. He did manage to acquire a limited knowledge of some of the martial arts and during basic training set the platoon record for stripping and reassembling a Bren gun. The only other thing Cuneo remembers learning was never to volunteer for anything. The lesson came from a sergeant of mature years who had completed his colour service and been due to go to the Reserve in September 1939. His extension of active service, he blamed on Hitler personally and gave vent to his spleen in the only way possible by discomforting the recruits in his charge. From a large repertoire he could produce seemingly innocuous questions to trap the unwary – "Any pianists among you lot?", or "Is there a good artist here?". Those foolhardy enough to answer in the affirmative found themselves either carrying a piano from the NAAFI to the Sergeants' Mess or whitewashing a less than fragrant latrine.

However, Cuneo did not have to endure this drollery for long. During his first leave from Osset he was contacted by a publishing house who wanted him to contribute to their popular 'How to Draw' series. They suggested he should do *Tanks and how to draw them* – a subject of which he was almost totally ignorant. Although at the time he had no way of knowing it, this book was to be the key to a career of great variety and success. On his return from leave he was given a posting order to go to Ripon for transfer to the Royal Engineers. Strings had been pulled. Almost every class of tank – Valentine, Matilda, Churchill, etc – was to be found at Ripon where they were being used for testing the new Bailey Bridge. He drew tanks inside and outside and from every angle, from morning till night. He loved every minute of it and became, and still is, an authority on tank recognition. His time with the Royal Engineers was very happy but he still hankered to be recognised as an official war artist. Many applications were made to the War Office, but to no avail. Then one day he was approached by a publicity firm who were handling a propa-ganda campaign for the Ministry of Information. He was asked to produce a series of large drawings for an exhibition in London showing the activities of the Resistance in occupied Europe. Agog with excitement at the prospect of being officially required to do what he did best, he was soon on his way to London. On the basis of a briefing by members of the Resistance, and with the help of sketches and notes they had made on the spot at the time, he got to work. Within three weeks 24 huge drawings were complete and a few days later 'The Unconquerable Soul' exhibition was opened at Charing Cross underground station.Then it was back to Ripon.

The undoubted success of the exhibition led to more work, this time for the Foreign Office depicting Nazi atrocities. The drawings, based on gruesome photographs, were printed as leaflets to be dropped over Germany and Italy to show the people there the horrors that were being perpetrated in their name. Terence Cuneo's reputation was now becoming widely known in military circles and his next assignment was with MI5 preparing highly secret assessments

'On the Strip-line'. 1943. (Courtesy the Imperial War Museum).

of harbour construction at possible invasion ports on the Continent. For the first time he felt he was making a real contribution to winning the war.

In 1944, Cuneo received a friendly but slightly critical letter from someone who had read and liked his *Tanks and how to draw them*. Cuneo agreed with the comments and, shortly afterwards, met the writer – a Mr George Garland. They got on well and learning of his aspirations, Garland offered an introduction to Sir William Russell Flint who in turn recommended Cuneo for work with the War Artists Advisory Committee, then under the direction of Sir Kenneth (later Lord) Clark. The first task he was given was a series of drawings of Churchill tank production at the Luton Car Works. The drawings now reside in the Imperial War Museum but the great interest shown in them when they were first seen led to an important series of aircraft

The assembly of Beaufighters.

commissions. Paintings of the Spitfire, Hurricane, Lancaster, Mosquito, Beaufighter and Wellington were completed, together with depictions of almost every engineering process involved in their manufacture. Around this time the publicity manager of the LNER happened to see a painting of Cuneo's at the London Sketch Club annual exhibition; the subject was an old Essex water mill. He was much taken with it and asked Cuneo if he would copy the work to the size of a 'double royal' poster. This led to Cuneo being asked to paint what was to become one his most famous posters – 'Giants Refreshed' – in the Doncaster paint shop. Further commissions were placed by the LMS and later by British Rail who charged Cuneo with the production of an entire set of major 'prestige' posters. Years later, Cuneo's work for British Rail was to be described by their Chairman as "a chronicle of the railways themselves" and in 1990 the artist received the rare and great compliment of having one of the latest 140 mph Class 91 electric locomotives named after him – the 'Terence Cuneo'.

Rolls-Royce Merlin/Griffon engines on the production line. Derby, 1944.
(Painted direct and finished on the spot – no photographs!)

In 1948 Lloyds of London were seeking an artist to depict the bustling throng of their Underwriting Room when they came across some of Cuneo's railway 'crowd scenes'. They realised that the search was over and he was invited to undertake the painting, which was warmly received and hung in the 1949 Royal Academy Exhibition. Some years later when it was known that the Queen (still yet to be crowned) had agreed to lay the foundation stone for Lloyds' new building, Cuneo was the natural choice to record the ceremony. Among the sitters for this canvas was Sir Terence Nugent of the Lord Chamberlain's office. One day he telephoned to ask if he might bring the Lord Chamberlain (Lord Scarborough) to Cuneo's studio. Cuneo naturally agreed but was hardly prepared for what took place at the meeting. After talking generalities for a while Lord Scarborough turned to Cuneo and asked "What would you say were I to invite you to paint the official picture of the coronation of the Queen in Westminster Abbey?" A dumbfounded Cuneo could only stammer "I'd say . . . Yes!"

That Herculean task was to be the springboard for more ceremonial and equestrian paintings, Royal portraits and military paintings of every sort. An already considerable reputation was even further enhanced and he found himself, in his own words, "In contact with the greatest in the land". This was the heady climax of a chain of events that began with that "friendly but slightly critical" letter from George Garland. Cuneo sometimes wonders what might have happened had he not bothered to answer it.

Cuneo's formal artistic association with the British Army dates from 1950 when a letter arrived asking him to record the presentation of colours to the Parachute Regiment's three regular battalions at Aldershot. The words seem to march off the page – "These will be the first colours to be presented to the Regiment and the occasion is therefore a notable one." Cuneo had suspected this from the opening sentence mentioning that the King was going to be there, but what he had not anticipated was the Army's tendency to rehearse everything in great detail to ensure an air of splendid spontaneity on the day. He recalls the occasion:

"First we plotted the ceremony on paper and then I attended a dress rehearsal at which Field Marshal Montgomery stood in for the King. When the parade was over everyone again took up the positions I wanted to paint them in – so that the whole sequence would be illustrated. At lunch in the mess afterwards I told the Field Marshal of the difficulties I would have to face on the day by being so far away from the actual scene. He appreciated the problem. Later he told me he had an idea – 'When you see the King and me leave the platform, come down from your "hide", make your way round the ground and come up to the saluting base. When I see you there I will get the King to look in the direction you require and then you can at least get a photo or two, what?' This struck me as a good scheme and I explained the direction in which I would like His Majesty to look.

"The great day came. During the early part of the parade there were showers but these cleared and the sun shone fitfully. I worked steadily as the ceremony progressed, concentrating on aspects I had not seen before – the crowded stands, the figures on the saluting base, the Queen's dress and that of the Lady-in-Waiting, the Royal Standard above the trees, the massed Colours draped over the drums and, in particular, the figures of the King and the Field Marshal. I noted additions in the ranks of the clergy and the groundsmen marking the boundaries of the parade. Finally the last colour was presented, the King turned and, with Monty, began to walk back to the saluting base. This was my cue. Leaving my paraphernalia in the care of an officer, I shinned down a ladder and set off. The distance was greater than I had thought. I had to skirt the entire parade ground, negotiate four sets of ropes, avoid dogs and prams whilst forcing my way through masses of people. Breathlessly, I rushed on, haunted by the fear that the march-past might begin and that I would be too late. As I panted up to the saluting base I was confronted by members of the Press. 'No nearer', they warned. 'It's all right' I snapped, 'It's been arranged'. Ahead, beside the base, I saw a flower box. It was on the edge of this that it had been agreed I should try to get the photograph. I clambered up, crushing some carnations, and got a shoeful of earth! I fiddled with the camera, focusing on two figures above me. Then, dishevelled and puffing like a grampus, I waited for a signal of recognition. Monty, although he'd promised to look out for me, was deep in conversation with the King and their backs were turned. Time was running out and still nobody on the saluting base looked in my direction. I was desperate and considered throwing a stone to attract attention when, at last, Monty turned and saw me. I gave a half wave and smiled. Monty nodding in the direction we had agreed on, spoke to the King who generously co-operated and kept still long enough for me to get several shots. And that was it. I went home entertaining mixed feelings about military parades."

As often happens when one hopes something will be absolutely perfect, the photographs turned out to be useless so Cuneo screwed up courage to ask for a sitting. Three weeks later found him in the Chinese Drawing Room at Buckingham Palace waiting for the King. This was his first Royal sitting and, indeed, the first time he had been inside the Palace. Double doors swung open. A footman announced "His Majesty is approaching". Cuneo pressed himself against the side of the doorway and swallowed hard. Suddenly, there was the King, a smiling figure coming forward with hand outstretched. Cuneo remembers every detail:

"I don't know whether I unconsciously expanded my mighty torso or whether the thing was loose anyway but, to my horror, I saw a shirt button fly off in an arc and land in the King's hand – a brilliant start! But in no time I was put completely at ease and the King's kindness to me during the time he posed is something I shall always remember. When

The Coronation of Her Majesty Queen Elizabeth II, Westminster Abbey, 2nd June 1953.

the work was finished he put his hand on my shoulder, 'Come with me, Cuneo, I'd like to show you something'. We walked down a long corridor and stopped in front of a huge canvas – the painting of his own coronation in 1937 by Frank Salisbury. He described various aspects of the work and asked me questions about an artist's problems in painting in such a scene. He even told me an amusing story about an incident that occurred during the ceremony.

"My mind has often gone back to this occasion. Of all the hundreds of paintings in the Palace why did the King take me to that particular one? Neither of us could have known that one day I would be chosen to paint the coronation of his daughter as Queen Elizabeth II."

The King featured in one other painting of Cuneo's that year when he dined in the Royal Artillery Mess at Woolwich on 7 December 1950. The Master Gunner, Field Marshal Viscount Alanbrooke, speaking at this glittering occasion declared that it added a memorable page to the history of the Royal Regiment of Artillery, being the first time a King and Colonel-in-Chief had dined with the Regiment. But when he saw the preliminary sketch Alanbrooke had some doubts. "Cuneo" he said, "you've shown the King as the smallest man in the picture!" Trying not to sound patronising, Cuneo explained "Unfortunately, Master Gunner, the problem is unavoidable in paintings like this of banquets and State occasions. It's always the same; the most important people must of necessity be in the background, otherwise they cannot be shown full-face to the viewer. If we bring them to the foreground, where of course they will be bigger, they are bound to be shown three-quarter back view or, at best, in 'lost profile'. You'll agree? In the case of the King this would be quite unacceptable." Alanbrooke looked at the sketch again. "Humph" he said, "I suppose you're right."

During an ordinary guest night in the Mess the great Waterford chandeliers are switched on only when toasts are drunk. However, it was hardly feasible to paint the scene of the Royal dinner by candlelight, so arrangements were made on a subsequent guest night for the lights to remain on throughout the dinner. Together, these chandeliers throw out heat equivalent to thirty 1,000-watt fires. By the end of the dinner the officers felt they had spent the evening in a sauna. It was fine for Cuneo, up on scaffolding, painting away in an open-necked shirt and jeans, cool as a cucumber while the unfortunate Gunners were obliged to sweat it out in full mess-kit. He sensed his popularity waning as the evening wore on. After the initial work in the Mess, the Director of Music, Lieutenant-Colonel Geary, with members of the orchestra, complete with violins, harp, etc., the famous 'white waiters' in their Georgian livery and members of the Women's Royal Army Corps went to Cuneo's studio for foreground poses. Thus the St. Barbara's Day Dinner was completed.

There is no doubt that 1950 was a memorable year for Cuneo. It saw the beginning of a special relationship with the Army that was to become ever closer with the passing of the years. Cuneo admired those who followed the profession of arms in the service of their country – their self-discipline, their zest for life and their great sense of comradeship. As he got to know them he began to appreciate things he had never seriously thought about – like what the Colours mean to a regiment. When he painted the presentation of their Colours, the history of the Parachute Regiment was short but its achievements in a comparatively few years had been heroic and the sense of pride in the soldiers who paraded that day in Aldershot, in the presence of their Monarch, was almost tangible. Cuneo was to paint many more Colour presentations and always he would sense the great pride in belonging, the belief every soldier held that his was the best regiment in the army. Asked what he does, a soldier will rarely admit to being in the Army. Rather he will proclaim himself a Gunner, a Sapper, a Cherrypicker, a Green Jacket, or one of the many other famous names that give a unique identity.

Cuneo found that he shared with soldiers a highly developed and robust sense of humour, which has

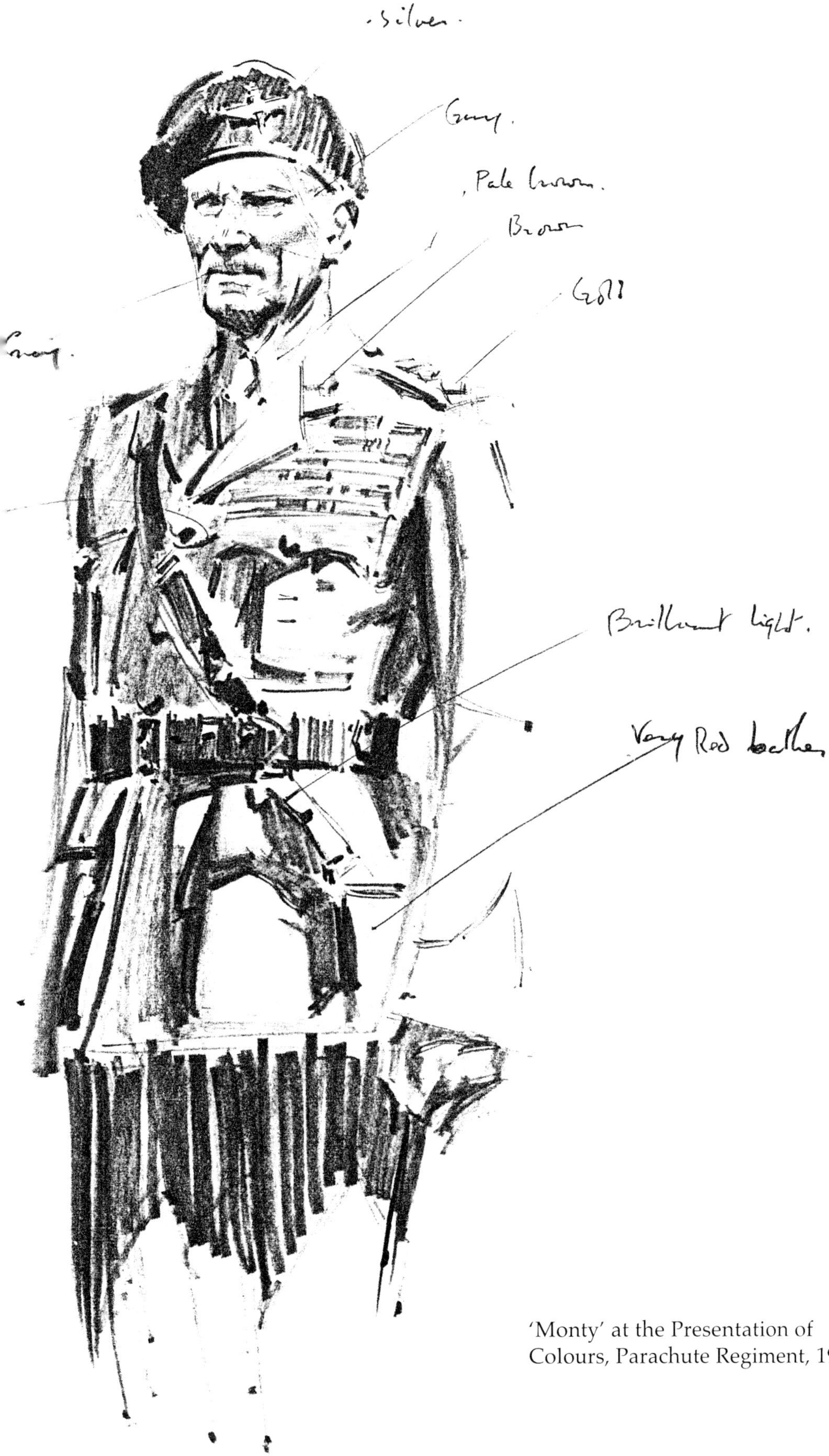

'Monty' at the Presentation of Colours, Parachute Regiment, 1950.

sometimes been said to be the British Army's single most effective weapon. In World War I the German General Staff produced a training pamphlet to teach their soldiers how to acquire a sense of humour and as an example of what made Tommy Atkins laugh included a Bruce Bairnsfather cartoon. 'Old Bill' is sitting by a wall, in which an enemy shell has blown a huge hole, and smoking his pipe. A young soldier new to the Western Front, asks "What made that 'ole?". Old Bill replies "Mice". The German handbook helpfully added the footnote "It was not mice. It was a shell."

As with soldiers, the way of the artist does not always go smoothly. In 1966 Cuneo was working on a painting for the Welsh Guards of the Queen and the Duke of Edinburgh leaving the Palace for Trooping the Colour. Both had already posed on horseback and the Queen had consented to a final sitting at the Palace, chiefly for details of head and shoulders. She sat elevated on a dais at the exact height she would be when mounted on her horse 'Imperial'. At the close, Cuneo asked if, at some later date, he might see her uniform for details of medals and regimental and other insignia. Her Majesty agreed and referred him to her dresser who promised to have the full uniform, including head-dress, arranged on a dummy. On the appointed day Cuneo entered the Pine Room to see, immaculate on an iron frame, the 'Queen' in full uniform. All he had to do before starting was lift the figure to the top of the dais to get the right perspective. Gripping the dummy firmly he put a foot on the first step, but he hadn't realised how top-heavy the thing was. Before he knew it he was off balance and he and the dummy were heeling over at a perilous angle. Desperately trying to straighten up, he tripped on the next step and came off the dais in a tottering run. At that very moment he glanced at the french window to see a knot of staring people pointing at him. His mind reeled as he imagined them running for the police – "Hurry! There's a maniac attacking the Queen!" Sweating profusely and red in the face, he grounded the dummy and dashed to draw the curtains across the long window. Now he could resume, in privacy, his struggles to get 'Her Majesty' on to her horse.

For many years Cuneo has enjoyed a cordial relationship with the Royal Regiment of Artillery – the Gunners – and has made many close friends among them, especially Martin Farndale, who was a young major when they first met and who went on to be Commander-in-Chief, British Army of the Rhine. General Sir Martin Farndale is now Master Gunner, St. James's Park. He was instrumental in getting Cuneo to paint a number of outstanding pictures for the Royal Artillery. Apart from the first commission already mentioned, there have been several paintings of actions in which the Gunners played a leading role. These include 'The Eagle Troop at the Battle of Hyderabad', 'The Battle of the Imjin River' and 'The Battle of Monte Cassino'. The latter two are in the RA Mess at Woolwich. As always, Cuneo took great pains to research these actions. When he could find gunners who had actually taken part he elicited every relevant detail they could recall and the end result is work as authentic as possible. The Corps of Royal Engineers also commissioned several of his most notable military works and having been, albeit briefly, a sapper himself, he has a special affection for them – even their colonels who, according to Kipling, have sometimes been slandered as "Methodist, married or mad!"

As his association with the Army became closer it was all but inevitable that Cuneo would be asked to paint portraits of distinguished commanders. Not surprisingly, none made a greater impression on him than Field Marshal The Viscount Montgomery of Alamein – 'Monty'. His first encounter with Monty was in connection with the painting of the German surrender at Luneburg Heath in May 1945. When he began his portrayal of this historic event Cuneo could not help feeling that a unique opportunity had been missed to record the drama as it was unfolding. His own work, commissioned well after the War, could only be an interpretation based on a black and white photograph, whose only use was to establish the relative positions of the principal characters involved in

Sefton in his stall.

the formal surrender. He gave much thought to creating the tense atmosphere that he felt must have prevailed in the tent and when the painting was nearly three-quarters done he sought an appointment with the great man to get his views and borrow a tunic for the Field Marshal's many medals. In due course he was invited to Montgomery's house at Isington Mill in Hampshire. Monty studied the canvas for some time then, stabbing a finger at the officer shown on his right, said "The red tabs must come off that fellow – he was merely an interpreter. Had to have an interpreter there to tell the Germans exactly what they were going to hear from me!" Nervously, Cuneo interjected, "But in the photograph it's pretty clear he's an Army officer – I mean it's not just the red tabs is it? It's the whole uniform – and anyway he's wearing a pistol hoster." Monty was quite unmoved by photographic evidence, "No, the fellow's an interpreter. Very necessary to make my orders clear to these German chaps. Very necessary." Like many before him in encounters with the Field Marshal,

Cuneo decided it would not be prudent to argue, but when he got back to his studio he painted in the officer in question as the brigadier he was in fact.

Before leaving Isington Mill there was still the matter of borrowing Monty's tunic. The Field Marshal left the room and returned bearing a small framed set of medals. "Are these the ones you wore on the day, Sir?" asked Cuneo. "Yes, these are the ones," Monty answered. Cuneo hesitated, "But in the photo of the surrender I'm sure you had five rows – here there are only three." Monty showed not the slightest interest in this observation. "You won't go far wrong if you copy these," he assured him and the subject of Germans surrendering at Luneburg Heath was removed from the agenda as they adjourned for tea. Back at the studio Cuneo studied the photograph again very carefuly. There was no comparison between the medals the Field Marshal had shown him and those in the photo taken at the time which unmistakably comprised five rows. Feeling oddly disloyal, he applied a rainbow of bright colours to his canvas to show five rows of ribbons on the Field Marshal's chest and stood back form the picture. It looked right – just like the photograph. So why should he feel uneasy? The photo couldn't lie, could it? And Monty had been wrong about the interpreter. But how on earth could the indomitable Victor of Alamein possibly be wrong about his own medals? Cuneo sighed. If only the Field Marshal had worn a greatcoat . . . Some years later, in 1972 Terence Cuneo was to paint the portrait of Montgomery that is now recognized as one of his finest works.

This volume can only show a selection of the hundreds of military works that this fine artist has completed in his long career. Cuneo finds much personal satisfaction in his military paintings and uses his talents to bring practical help to soldiers and their dependants through his support of Army charities. When asked to sign prints of his work he usually requires that a donation be made to the Army Benevolent Fund and this generous habit has raised substantial sums to relieve hardship. He has also painted major works expressly for Army charity. Two well-known pictures have produced some £40,000 through the sale of prints, greeting cards and the auction of the original works.

The first picture was painted in 1982 and, called 'Outrage', it depicts a wounded horse. At 10 o' clock on the morning of Tuesday 20 July 1982, a troop of the Mounted Regiment of the Household Cavalry rode out from Knightsbridge Barracks to take over as Queen's Guard in Whitehall. It was a regular part of the colourful pageantry of the nation's capital, essential viewing for tourists and holiday-makers and a special treat for children come to town to see the Queen's horses and the Queen's men. Suddenly,

Her Royal Highness,The Princess Anne at the auction of the 'Outrage' painting, at the Royal Chelsea Hospital.

without warning, it became a slaughter. A terrorist bomb exploded killing four members of the Blues and Royals and maiming seven cavalry horses so badly they had to be shot.It was an appalling act of barbaric cruelty that evoked disgust and loathing for the perpetrators. It also brought forth a spontaneous, widespread expression of sympathy for all who had suffered, especially the families who had been bereaved. In a strange way one horse came to symbolise the tragedy. He was the most cruelly injured of the animals who survived – 40 severe wounds, including six 5-inch nails in his head – and his dignity in suffering was captured on the television news that evening. The reaction was incredible. It was as if the entire nation had adopted this one brave horse and made him the focus of sympathy for those whose lives had been destroyed by this terrible deed. The horse was called Sefton.

Cuneo was sickened by the news and, characteristically, wanted to do something about it – although he wasn't sure what. Having thought about the event, he became convinced that this poor, mutilated creature would be the fitting symbol of such a wicked act and that a portrait could perhaps raise money to help the bereaved families. Instinctively, he knew he had the title for his painting. He would call it 'Outrage'. With his objective clear there was only one way he could proceed – full steam ahead. He rang me at the Army Benevolent Fund and within the hour was driving his Bristol at breakneck speed to the stables at Knightsbridge Barracks. He didn't know which was Sefton's stall but then he saw hundreds of 'get well' cards stuck on an enormous board and realised he'd arrived. He remembers:

"I went into the loose box. The sight was heart-rending. He stood there, forlorn, listless, neck lowered, one hind leg rested, with a coat from which all the proud gloss had been brutally erased. The wounds from the nails which had ripped his flesh were dreadful, but the worst was the still open gash that had severed the jugular vein. A man had stuffed his shirt into this gaping hole to get the horse back to the barracks alive. I was shown where a nail had pinned his bridle to his head. I could scarcely hold back the tears.

"Sefton was in too much pain to leave his box so I did my best to make a rough sketch crammed against the loose-box wall. When I got home I was uncomfortably convinced that *something* was lacking in the composition. As I pondered, I thought I knew what was missing – the *human* contact. The next morning I returned to the barracks to find that, miraculously, Sefton was showing small signs of improvement and could actually move outside his box. When I saw him standing in the sunshine, a loose halter in the hand of his farrier, I knew this was what the subject needed. The presence of the farrier in his long leather apron established an atmosphere of compassion and concern for the animal's welfare. I set to work with a will. Officers of the regiment came to look over my shoulder and nodded approval. Finally, the mouse took up a respectful place in the background and I invited Gerald down for a preview. He was delighted and suggested making the unveiling a very special occasion indeed. He approached Princess Anne's secretary to see if she would consider coming as the guest of honour. She accepted and arrangements were made for a reception in the State Apartments of the Royal Hospital, Chelsea. What an evening it turned out to be!

"We had decided that the painting should be auctioned and taken steps to invite guests who were horse-lovers – easy; well-disposed to the welfare of soldiers and their families – easy; and rich – not so easy! I was concerned that the bidding might not take off and the painting would be knocked down for a couple of hundred. 'Don't worry', said Gerald, 'if it doesn't sell you can paint it over and use the canvas again.' I hoped he was joking. But I needn't have worried. The auction was held on 28 September. Before it began and to the delight of everyone present, Sefton himself appeared. The place buzzed with happy excitement. On 20 July he had been all but given up for dead, a battered horse only being kept alive by the skill of Noel Carding, the Household Cavalry's veterinary surgeon, and his own courage and determination.

Her Royal Highness,The Princess Anne at the unveiling of 'D-Day' at the National Army Museum, Chelsea.

And now, just over two months' later, he was like a frisky two-year old. He condescended to take a carrot or two from Princess Anne, who knew the protocol for feeding horses on formal occasions – and was the only one with ready access to a silver salver – but clearly he was in no mood to be upstaged by anyone. It was Sefton's night.

"The Princess accepted the working sketch I had done the day after the outrage and then we all moved inside for the auction. Lord Oaksey had agreed to be the auctioneer and quickly got everything under control with some lively banter. He made it clear that serious bidding was expected. In no time he was calling for three, four, five thousand pounds. A pause – someone said 'Six' and Oaksey started to say 'Going at six...', but then they charged again, seven, seven-five, eight, nine and through the barrier of ten thousand! Still it wasn't over – ten-five, eleven, eleven-five, twelve – 'Going at twelve thousand pounds...' said John Oaksey and that was the cue for the great philanthropist, Raphael Djanogly, timing his bid to a nicety to catch the auctioneer's eye and say, rather quietly, 'Twelve thousand five hundred pounds.' The painting was his."

Cuneo could hardly contain his pleasure that his painting of a brave animal had raised such a handsome sum to help those who had suffered through the cowardly deed of 20 July. Truly good had triumphed over evil.

Perhaps the final word on this dastardly act should be left to Sir Alastair Burnet who wrote at the time "...in Ireland, where they certainly love horses, they took it personally as a crime against their country. So the murderers had miscalculated again. Sefton, scarred but serene once more, and apparently indestructible, had seen them off." (Sefton died on 9 July 1993).

The second important picture was commissioned by the Army Benevolent Fund in 1984. It was 40 years after D-Day and it had been suggested that a souvenir be produced to mark the occasion and at the same time raise money for Army Benevolence. Eventually, it was decided that Cuneo should be asked to do a large canvas to capture something of the drama of D-Day – 6 June 1944. Cuneo had reservations.He was being asked to portray a scene of which he knew nothing at first hand. He could neither include everything (it would have to be of Bayeux tapestry proportion), nor choose one particular incident. The painting would have to be a composite with the attendant risk that in seeking to please everybody he might end up pleasing nobody; but he could never resist a challenge.

Having read what he could and talked to many old soldiers who had taken part, he sought the advice of Gerald Landy who suggested that they visit the Imperial War Museum to see what photographs they had of the invasion. The staff at the Museum could not have been more helpful. There were ex-servicemen amongst them who showed the keenest interest in the project. Hundreds of photographs, taken shortly after the landings, were removed from countless boxes and when these had been studied hundreds more were produced. Although these were not action photographs but taken during lulls in the fighting, they nevertheless proved invaluable in identifying the landing craft, armoured and other vehicles, and much of the equipment used in the action. There were also enough pictures of the fighting men to reveal something of the fatigue of battle. At first, some of the photos seemed surprising: chaplains, well up at the sharp end, sharing a joke and a mug of tea. But that wasn't really surprising at all. That was where the chaplains usually were, bringing good cheer in their special earthy way, knowing the words that hearten when fear and danger chill the spirit. As if for light relief, there were photographs of bicycles, GS, classic transport of the company runner from time immemorial, somehow giving reassurance that on an invasion beach in Normandy or in the company lines at Aldershot, the ordinary routine of life goes on.

Cuneo made numerous small sketches and was allowed to borrow photos of major equipment. After three days of detailed work he returned to his studio, greatly warmed by the help and enthusiasm he had found at the museum and confident that he could capture the essence of D-Day on a single canvas. It took some weeks to finish the painting. It was impressive. He called it simply 'D-Day – 6 June 1944'. The National Army Museum seemed the perfect place to unveil the picture and, once again, Princess Anne agreed to adjust some of her other commitments to fit in an extra task. Thus the launch of 'D-Day' became a royal event.

A substantial dais was set up in the main picture gallery and permission was given for spotlights and recordings of small-arms fire to be brought in. Cuneo wanted the occasion to go with a bang – literally. A brief rehearsal was held under the disdainful gaze of assorted noble commanders of the 18th century, who looked down on the scene from their gilded frames, and on the morning of the brilliantly sunny day that followed the Princess uncovered 'D-Day' to public gaze for the first time. She showed great interest in the work and its purpose, and seemed pleased to have found the mouse without anyone having to tell her where it was.

A number of bids were received for the painting but no one was surprised when it was announced that the successful one was again from Mr Raphael Djanogly at £13,500. A limited edition of large, fine-art quality prints signed by the artist, supplemented by a larger unsigned edition, went on sale.

To bring the story of the artist's military paintings up to date, he completed in 1991 two major works showing aspects of the Gulf War. One, called 'The Basrah Road', was commissioned by the Queen's Royal Irish Hussars and shows some of the Regiment's tanks waiting to move to that road to cut off the withdrawal of the Iraqis from Kuwait City during the closing stages of the Gulf War on 28 February 1991. The ceasefire came into effect at 08.00 hours that morning.

The second, called 'Desert Storm', depicts Challenger tanks in a typical battle scene in the Gulf. His studies for this were done on the tank training ground at Bovington.
There is a counterpart painting to Cuneo's by his friend Frank Wootton, showing RAF aircraft taking off for a bombing raid on Iraqi positions. Lord Rothermere was instrumental in

arranging the painting of both works and HRH The Duke of Kent formally accepted the pictures from him at the offices of the Royal Air Force Benevolent Fund on 13 December 1991. The paintings were given to raise money for the Army and RAF Benevolent Funds.

In the pages that follow, Cuneo has made a selection of the military paintings that he feels are most representative of his achievements in this field. He would not be so foolhardy as to indicate which are his personal favourites for he cherishes the friendship of every regiment and corps.

More than 78 years have passed since a small boy first coloured a drawing of imaginary soldiers going to war. In that time Cuneo has painted many pictures of the real thing and the passing of the years has strengthened the affection he has always had for the British soldier. The feeling is mutual – each has a special place in his heart for the other, Cuneo is the soldier's painter. He and his mouse belong to the Army.

Now in his mid-eighties, Cuneo still paints every day. He shows little sign of slowing down, no loss of enthusiasm, no lack of alertness. The hand seems as steady as ever and the eye as clear – but best of all – the sense of fun is still as lively as can be.

Terence Cuneo remains the most complete military painter of the age.

Terence Cuneo talking to a Challenger tank crew, at Bovington.

Raising the Regiment–The Green Howards

November 1688.

Colonel Francis Luttrell in the courtyard of Dunster Castle in November 1688 signing on and issuing arms to his men prior to their departure for Exeter in support of Prince William of Orange (William III). Wearing the Luttrell livery of blue, lined with yellow, they were known as Luttrell's Regiment and took precedence as the first regiment to be raised in England in William's cause. (Colonel Walter Luttrell, a descendant of Francis, gave Dunster Castle to the National Trust in the 1970s.)

The regiment first saw action in 1690 at the Battle of the Boyne in Ireland but soon found itself in Marlborough's campaigns in Flanders where it won, at great cost, its first battle honour – Malplaquet – in 1709. In 1744 it was back in Flanders. The Regimental Colonel was General Charles Howard, son of the Earl of Carlisle and, in the custom of the time, the Regiment bore its Colonel's name – 'Howard's Regiment'. In one campaign they were brigaded with another regiment whose colonel was also named Howard, so to avoid confusion each added the colour of its uniform facings to its title, one becoming The Green Howards and the other, The Buff Howards. The nickname 'Green Howards' stuck and survived until 1920 when it became part of the Regiment's official title - The Green Howards (Alexandra Princess of Wales's Own Yorkshire Regiment).

The association with Yorkshire dates from 1782 when it received the title 'The 19th (or First Yorkshire North Riding Regiment) of Foot'. The reference to Alexandra reflects a special relationship with the House of Denmark which began in 1875 when Alexandra, Princess of Wales (formerly of the Royal House of Denmark and later Queen Alexandra) presented new colours to the Regiment. She designed their cap badge, incorporating the Cross of Denmark, her personal cypher and her coronet. In 1914 as Queen Alexandra, this much-loved lady became their first Colonel-in-Chief and when she died in 1925 she had been closely associated with her regiment for 50 years. The link with the Danish Royal House was renewed in 1942 when her son-in-law King Haakon VII of Norway (born Prince Carl of Denmark) became Colonel-in-Chief. On his death the appointment was taken up by his son, King Olav V, and when he died he was succeeded by his son, King Harald – the present Colonel-in-Chief.

In the 300 years since it was raised the Regiment has won 90 battle honours of which 30 are emblazoned on the Regimental Colours. In 1781 they fought in the American War of Independence. They distinguished themselves in the Crimea (1853-56) at Inkerman, Sevastopol (two VCs) and Alma, where they stormed the Great Redoubt. Every year on 20 September the Regiment celebrates Alma Day and traditionally beats the drums that were captured from the Russians in that battle. In World War I they won 12 Victoria Crosses (including four at the Somme) and gained 56 battle honours. In World War II, two of their battalions were first to land in Normandy on D Day and by the end of that War they had won three Victoria Crosses (including the only one awarded on D Day itself), 177 other awards for gallantry and earned 25 battle honours.

Raising the Regiment – The King's Own Scottish Borderers. March 1689.

Originally the 25th Foot, the Regiment was raised in Edinburgh on 18 March 1689 by David Leslie, 3rd Earl of Leven, for the defence of the city against the Jacobites during the 'Glorious Revolution' that brought William of Orange to England. Records show that the Regiment was completely recruited to a strength of 1,000 men within the space of two hours.

They were soon required for active service and at the Battle of Killiecrankie underwent their baptism of fire against the rebel Highlanders led by Claverhouse. Recognition of the fighting spirit of Leven's Edinburgh Regiment came at once in the spontaneous conferment on it, by the Provost of Edinburgh, of the exclusive privilege to recruit by beat of drum in the city on any day, except Sunday, without first asking the permission of the Lord Provost. A further privilege was conferred later, which remains to this day, of marching through the City of Edinburgh with bayonets fixed and Colours flying.

In 1782 the historic title of 'The Edinburgh Regiment' was dropped and that of 'The Sussex Regiment' adopted. King George III honoured the Regiment in 1805 by raising it to the status of a Royal Regiment and changing its title to 'The King's Own Borderers'. The change of title to 'The King's Own Scottish Borderers' was officially approved in 1887, during the reign of Queen Victoria.

Cuneo has depicted the scene at Holyrood Abbey at nightfall on 18 March 1689 when 1,000 men answered the call to arms. The Earl of Leven and the Muster Master watch from horseback while the clerk lists the men and issues the first day's pay. The yellow ribbon on the arm of the recruit was issued as a mark of recognition until uniform could be provided.

· CUNEO ·
DECEMBER '80

The Battle of Killiecrankie, 1689.

Shortly after being raised by Lord Leven for the defence of Edinburgh against the Jacobites, the 25th Regiment of Foot was sent to confront a force of rebel Scottish Highlanders led by John Graham of Claverhouse, Viscount Dundee, known to his followers as 'Bonnie Dundee' and to the Covenanters he had for years cruelly suppressed as 'Bloody Clavers'.

Battle was joined at the Pass of Killiecrankie in the Tayside region of Scotland. The rebels had the best of the day, although Claverhouse himself was killed. This bloody encounter was the first action that Lord Leven's Regiment took part in. They fought bravely and withdrew only when directly commanded to do so and then 'in splendid order'. The Regiment exists to this day as The King's Own Scottish Borderers.

When he painted this magnificent picture, Cuneo found that it only takes two Scotsmen to make a battle.
He recalls:
"Looking back on this 17th century affray in the wilds of Scotland, I remember that just two soldiers of the King's Own Scottish Borderers posed for every single figure in the picture! One of them in the uniform of the Regiment and the other, as a wild clansman complete with kilt and claymore. These two fellows were great. Completely uninhibited, they threw themselves into the 'battle' with astonishing vigour. In fact, at one point things got so heated that I thought the King's man was going to get a dirk through his neck, and on another occasion the hand-to hand fighting was so realistic I was forced to intervene – as much for my own safety as for theirs. So if my picture conveys the reality of this grim battle, a deal of credit must go to my two lusty warrior-models."

FEBRUARY

The Battle of Hyderabad

North West India. 24 March 1843.

After General Sir Charles Napier defeated the Ameers (tribal chiefs) at Meeanee early in 1843, the Ameer Sheen Mohammed fled and over the next few months collected some 10,000 men in the Sind desert. On 24 March 1843, Napier's army of 5,000 met Mohammed's force at Dubba, near Hyderabad. 1st Troop, Bombay Horse Artillery (now N Battery – 'The Eagle Troop') were not part of this force but arrived just in time for the subsequent battle.

The fierce encounter shown in Cuneo's painting was fought in a temperature of 110 degrees and lasted three hours. When it ended Mohammed had lost between 6,000 to 8,000 men; the British 270. Napier stated: "The battle was decided by 1st Troop Bombay Horse Artillery and Her Majesty's 22nd Regiment (the Cheshire Regt)". After the battle the Governor-General of India directed that the 1st Troop "shall hereafter... in addition to all other decorations or inscriptions upon its appointments, bear the eagle."

To this day N Battery celebrates 24 March as 'Hyderabad Day'. The painting shows the dramatic moment in the battle when the commander of 1st Troop, Major Leslie (mounted in the foreground), galloped his Troop across the front of the infantry (the Cheshire Regiment on the right of the picture) and brought them crashing into action close to the enemy. He ordered Lieutenant Smith to go forward to find new gun positions but he was cut down and this can be seen in the distance on the left. The guns were five 6-pounders and one 12-pounder howitzer. The picture today is with N Battery now part of 3rd Regiment, Royal Horse Artillery.

Cuneo recalls: "This painting proved a brute to compose. The more the battle was explained to me the more baffled I became. There was so much to get in, and yet I knew that to achieve something that would stand on its own merits and 'read' well, a degree of simplicity was essential. I explained to members of the Regiment that the layout I had in mind was the only possible way in which the subject could be made to work as after all it was the guns that were of paramount importance and everthing else must be subsidiary to them. Here I had an unexpected stroke of luck. The Rotunda at Woolwich had nothing to offer apart from a howitzer of roughly the period, but as I was leaving the museum some model guns were being unloaded from a car. They were perfect - exactly the right period and with superb detail. Manna from heaven! I made studies of these 12-inchmodels in the various positions they cocupied in my composition and went on my way highly satisfied. Incidentally it was interesting to observe that apparently in those days limbers carried but one pair of shafts. This left the other 'wheeler' attached by traces alone like the other four horses."

CUNEO
OCTOBER 1990

Major Henry Clifford, VC

Inkerman, 5 November 1854.

The Crimean War (1854-56) between Russia and the allied powers of Britain, France, Turkey and Sardinia was one of the worst prepared campaigns that Britain ever embarked on. Organisation for administration and logistics was almost non-existent and of the 19,600 British losses 15,700 died from disease. The situation would have been even worse but for the selfless devotion of Florence Nightingale and her nurses who battled against dreadful conditions and official apathy to provide decent standards of nursing care for the sick and wounded.

The most famous military exploit of the War was the Charge of the Light Brigade at Balaclava on 25 October 1854. Though heroic, it was one of the greatest ever military disasters. A futile and suicidal cavalry charge was made through a valley overlooked on three sides by Russian guns. The French General Bosquet watched the charge in disbelief – "C'est magnifique mais ce n'est pas la guerre". Only ten days after Balaclava, the Battle of Inkerman took place. The Russians attacked Inkerman Ridge, occupied by the British, and were repulsed.

Major (later Major General) Henry Clifford was aide-de-camp to Major-General Sir George Buller, Commander of the Light Division, thoughout the Crimean War. Clifford, on horseback, accompanied the 77th Regiment in their charge at Inkerman in the early morning of 5 November 1854.This extract from Clifford's letter to his relations and friends the following day describes the incident portrayed in the painting:

". . . I saw the enemy in great numbers in our front, about 15 yards from us; it was a moment or two before I could make General Buller believe that they were Russians. 'In God's name, ' I said, 'fix bayonets and charge'. He gave the order and in another moment we were hand to hand with them. Our line was not long enough to prevent the Russians out-flanking our left, which was unperceived by the 77th who rushed on with the exception of about a dozen, who, struck by the force on our left and who saw me taking out my revolver, halted with me.

" 'Come on', I said, 'my lads!' and the brave young fellows dashed in amongst the astonished Russians, bayoneting them in every direction. One of the bullets in my revolver had partly come out and prevented it revolving and I could not get it off. The Russians fired their pieces off within a few yards of my head, but none touched me. I drew my sword and cut off one man's arm who was in the act of bayoneting me and a second, seeing it, turned round and was in the act of running out of my way, when I hit him over the back of the neck and made him dead at my feet. About 15 of them threw down their arms and gave themselves up and the remainder ran back and fell into the hands of the 77th returning from the spendid charge they had made and were killed or taken prisoners.

"Out of the small party with me (12), six men were killed and three wounded, so my escape was wonderful."

Cuneo remembers: "The great grandson of this brave officer posed for every single character in my picture. Somehow Robert had gleaned, from heaven knows where, a shako, various belts, bits of uniform both Russian and British, a contemporary sword and a rifle with bayonet. Thus armed and with vast enthusiasm, we fell to with a will. The majority of the foot poses went along smoothly enough but the tricky part was getting a good action pose of fighting on horseback. I decided to drag my Western saddle out into the garden and rig it up on a narrow brick wall. Getting the gallant 'Clifford' onto a 'horse' barely four inches in width rapidly descended into slap-stick comedy. However, after frequent collapses I had the intrepid rider with sword upraised more or less in the position I wanted. It was chaotic, but it worked."

FEBRUARY 1986

Corporal Philip Smith

The Leicestershire Regiment, winning the Victoria Cross during an assault on the Great Redan, Sebastopol, 1855.

Despite harsh conditions and poor maintenance, the soldiers in the Crimea fought bravely and there were many individual acts of great heroism. In 1856, Queen Victoria instituted the Victoria Cross, to be awarded only for conspicuous gallantry in the face of the enemy. Struck from metal taken from Russian cannon captured at Sebastopol, the simple bronze cross bears the words 'For Valour' and is worn suspended from a plain crimson ribbon. It is Britain's supreme award for bravery, taking precedence over all other decorations.

One of the earliest recipients of the Victoria Cross was Corporal (later Sergeant) Philip Smith of the 17th Regiment of Foot (later the Leicestershire Regiment). Born in Lurgan, Country Armagh, Ireland in 1825, he went to the Crimea with his Regiment and took part in attacks on the Great Redan (Russian fortifications). His brave deed was described thus:

"On 18 June 1855, in the Crimea, Corporal Smith went out repeatedly in front of the advanced trenches against the Great Redan, under heavy fire, after the column had retired from the assault, and brought in wounded comrades."

This brave man retired to Ireland at the end of his military service, and died at Harold's Cross, Dublin on 16 January 1906.

During this research, Cuneo unearthed an interesting and little known fact. During this period in military history, it was only officers who wore scarlet. Privates and non-commissioned officers were dressed in a coarser, red-brick material. It was unique to the Guards Regiments to have every man in scarlet tunic.

CUNEO
SEPTEMBER
1962

Sergeant, US 7th Cavalry

The uniform dates from 1876, the year of Custer's Last Stand. The brand, K7, on the horse's rump indicates K Troop, 7th Cavalry.

On 25 June 1876 during the Battle of Little Big Horn, Montana, Major-General George A. Custer, famous American Civil War hero and Indian-fighter, led some 225 men of the crack US 7th Cavalry in a foolhardy attack on a force of Sioux and Cheyenne Indians commanded by the great Sioux leader, Sitting Bull. By the end of the bloody encounter, which lasted little more than one hour, Custer and his heavily outnumbered troops had been annihilated. Only a few of their horses remained alive. The total absence of survivors shrouded this bold but ill-conceived action in an aura of mystery, serving to create an heroic legend out of a military disaster.

Not long after the actual event, re-enactments of 'Custer's Last Stand' began to feature in the Wild West Shows of Colonel 'Buffalo Bill' Cody and others. Such presentations remain popular to this day and Cuneo, a great admirer of the American West, often appeared in modern versions.

Cuneo comments: "Although the man in this painting never had to face Crazy Horse and his braves, he and I have many times ridden in Billy Smart's Circus, shooting at Sitting Bull and his Indians. Hardly as dramatic as the real thing perhaps, but tremendous fun for all that."

The Last Despatch

Khartoum, 15 December 1884.

Charles George Gordon was commissioned into the Royal Engineers in 1852 at the age of 19. After service in the Crimean War he was sent to China where he suppressed the Taiping rebellion in the Chinese War of 1860, acquiring the sobriquet 'Chinese Gordon'. Between 1877 and 1879 he was Governor of the Sudan. Service in India, China, the Cape and Palestine followed but he was ordered back to the Sudan in 1884 to rescue the British garrisons who were under attack by Sheik Mohammed Ahmed (the Mahdi). Instead he found himself besieged by the Mahdi's army in Khartoum.

Cuneo's painting shows General Gordon handing over his journal to a Turkish officer from the paddle steamer 'Bordein' on the 15th December with instructions to get the despatches into British hands with all speed. A relief expedition under General Garnet Wolseley arrived on 28 January 1885 to find that, after a siege of ten months, Khartoum had been captured - and Gordon killed - two days before.

In an age of colonial administrators of the highest quality Gordon was outstanding. His achievements captured the imagination of the country and brought him fame that bordered on the legendary. His violent death shocked the nation. Queen Victoria blamed Prime Minister Gladstone: "The news from Khartoum is frightful, and to think that all this might have been prevented and many precious lives saved by earlier action is too frightful." The incident contributed to the fall of Gladstone's government but secured a permanent place in British history for 'Gordon of Khartoum'.

Cuneo remembers: "Old Bordein, I believe, still exists in some form or other. Indeed, she was a pretty weathered old craft even in 1884, her decks and superstructure protected by rows of railway sleepers and her funnel liberally punctured by rifle bullets. I was lent the General's actual journal to work from, the one shown being handed over so dramatically on that fateful December day."

The Ambush at Sanna's Post

Boer War, 1900.

This painting shows the havoc, as visualised by Cuneo after reading regimental histories and citations. No less than four VCs were awarded to 'Q' Battery for gallantry in getting their guns into action when ambushed by a thousand Boers concealed behind the ridge of a dried-out donga (a dried-out water course), near Bloemfontein, in 1900. One of the 12-pounders used at that time was taken from the Rotunda Museum at Woolwich and was placed in the open for the artist, but not a single gunner could be found who knew how to operate it! However, the study of a contemporary instruction manual solved the problem and by the time Cuneo went to Woolwich to make his studies, four men had been trained and knew exactly what to do.

It was after this South African battle, where gunners had to face deadly accurate rifle fire from the Boers, that it occurred to the powers that be, that perhaps it would be a sound notion to fit some sort of shield on the guns, thus affording the crews a measure of protection from small arms fire. On the other hand, they argued, one shouldn't coddle the fellows! Thus was born the gun shield.

'Q' (Sanna's Post) Battery is very much alive today in 5th Regiment and still celebrates the day when it displayed so much bravery under fire.

·MUNRO·
FEBRUARY·1975

Saving the Guns at Le Cateau

26 August 1914.

This magnificent painting shows Captain Reynolds and Drivers Luke and Drain saving the guns of 37th Battery from under the very eyes of German infantry towards the end of the battle. One of the teams was brought down and Drain caught Luke's whip as he threw it in the air. All three were to be awarded the Victoria Cross for their gallantry. 37th Battery is now 97th (Le Cateau) Battery so that their heroism shall never be forgotten. This picture was painted in 1969.

Sergeant Alfred Knight, VC

2/8th (City of London) Bn, The London Regiment (Post Office Rifles), winning the Victoria Cross at Ypres. 20 September 1917.

The small Belgian town of Ypres ("Wipers" as it was known to the British Army) lies in West Flanders. It was the centre of some of the greatest and bloodiest battles of World War I. The Menin Gate, erected at nearby Menin in 1927, is a memorial to the thousands of British soldiers who lost their lives in the fighting at Ypres.

The 2/8th Battalion of The London Regiment was in action there in 1917. Sergeant Knight was a platoon sergeant. On 20 September 1917 at Alberta Section, Ypres, his platoon was pinned down by very heavy fire from an enemy machine-gun post. Rushing through our own barrage, he charged the enemy position and captured it single-handed. He went on to perform several further acts of conspicuous bravery, showing no regard for his personal safety.

All the platoon officers of the company having fallen casualty before the first objective was reached, this brave NCO took command not only of his own men but of those from the other platoons who had lost their officers.
His energy in consolidating and reorganising was untiring, and his leadership a source of tremendous inspiration.
He was awarded the Victoria Cross.

Sergeant Knight was later commissioned as a Second Lieutenant. After the War he returned to his home town of Birmingham.

Lieutenant John Cridland Barrett, VC

1/5th Bn. The Leicestershire Regiment leading an attack on an enemy trench, which won him the Victoria Cross. Pontruet, France, 24 September 1918.

In smoke and darkness and uncertain of his position, Lieutenant John Cridland Barrett found himself advancing on an enemy trench containing several machine-guns. Rallying all available men, he charged the nearest group of guns and, in spite of being wounded, personally knocked out two guns, inflicting many casualties. He was seriously wounded twice more in leading his men back to the battalion.

Cuneo recalls: "This picture was built up from drawings made at one of my favourite stamping grounds – Oxshott Heath in Surrey. Similar locations have served me well for much of my army work. But it is one thing to sketch from models in the calm light of day, quite another to convert those sketches into a context of raging night, torn by smoke and flame to convey something of the horror that John Barrett faced that night in 1918.

"On a lighter note, however, when we were getting the rifles, scuttle-helmets and machine guns from the truck for the Barrett picture, a little old lady approached. She had a rather portly, over-fed dachshund on a scarlet lead, and with her free hand, she pointed a trembling finger at the machine-gun. "I do hope you have no intention of firing that noisy thing' she spluttered, 'Mitzi suffers so dreadfully with her nerves, you know'."

The Last Stand of the 5th (Gibraltar) Battery, Royal Artillery. May 1918.

On the night of 26-27 May 1918, 5th Battery's gun position came under attack. At 07.00 hours the enemy forced their way onto the position. The Battery Commander and the two subalterns rallied the surviving men and with Lewis gun and rifles attempted to beat off the attack, but were overpowered. Only four gunners survived.

"That bald official statement bears little relation to the visual significance of what I was putting on canvas.
It was only when I stood back from the finished work to assess the picture's merit that the grim realisation of what I had created began to sink in. Suddenly, I felt I could hear the ghastly din of battle, see the grey horde of helmeted, masked figures advancing relentlessly through the smoke and gas, know what it was to stand surrounded and know that death would come this very instant."

The painting is still with 5th Battery, 14th Regiment, Royal Artillery. The Battery is now part of the Allied Mobile Force.

The Reverend Theodore Bayley Hardy, VC, DSO, MC, Chaplain to the Forces (4th Class).

The picture shows Theodore Bayley Hardy being invested with the Victoria Cross by King George V in 1918. Bayley Hardy joined the Royal Army Chaplains Department in 1916 and during the course of 11 months ministry on the Western Front was awarded the MC, DSO and VC. He died of wounds on 18 October 1918, within two days of his 55th birthday.

The black armband worn by the King indicated his mourning for the Russian Imperial Family who had been assassinated in July 1918.

TERENCE • CUNEO •
SEPTEMBER • 1966 •

First Air Post. 1 March 1919.

An historic event. Cuneo's picture commemorates the arrival of the first scheduled air mail flight from England (Folkestone) to Germany (Cologne) after World War I.
A de Havilland DH9 of the RAF, with machine gun removed, has its cargo of mail unloaded at Cologne and checked by a corporal of the Royal Engineers' Postal Section. The famous cathedral can be seen in the background between the aircraft's wings. Painted March 1978.

H
5567

To Russia with Love

Mail from home being unloaded near Archangel for men of the British Army of Occupation in Russia 1919. (Painted June 1978).

Cuneo recalls his research for this painting:

"So many things had to be checked. Russian and British First World War uniforms, the type of shaggy little pony the Russians used, the harness with the characteristic, decorative 'arch' above the horse; station buildings, wagons, and, of course, the locomotive. I learnt that at this time and earlier, Russian engines enjoyed a wealth of individual expression both in colour and design. Indeed, it was not unknown to see a bright pink locomotive in service, alongside others painted in greens, browns and scarlet, whilst some even boasted a portrait of Lenin on the tender. Wheels, too, were brilliantly coloured and engines often lined-out with ornate extravagance. My engine, alas, does not sport such kaleidoscopic indulgences. She is merely a work-horse, but nevertheless, displays a feature which has always intrigued me on Russian locomotives - the ship-like hand-rail which encompasses the boiler from cab-side to buffer-beam. I delved and finally discovered the reason. It seems that years ago a fireman fell from a moving locomotive and was killed. The Tsar, apparently upset by the tragedy, ordered that in future every engine should be equipped with a stout double rail fixed around all running boards to avoid any further casualties. The custom has remained ever since."

TERENCE CUNEO
JUNE 1978

Lawrence of Arabia

The Brough v. the Bristol Race.

One evening in the mid-1920s Colonel T. E. Lawrence, then serving in the RAF as Aircraftman Shaw, rode his beloved Brough Superior SS 100 motorcycle from the RAF Cadet College at Cranwell towards Lincoln. Soon he noticed a Bristol fighter from the neighbouring aerodrome flying low overhead and a race ensued. Lawrence relates in his autobiographical memoir *The Mint* how:

"The Brough, with much bumping and swaying, was more than a match for the Bristol and easily took the lead. Slowing to 90 then slowing down again, I finally waved the Bristol past, only to accelerate again, take the lead anew and maintain it. At journey's end, 14 miles from camp, the Bristol gave best to the Brough, banked and made for home, the pilot waving his acknowledgements."

The race illustrates Lawrence's passion for George Brough's motorcycles and the love of speed that fired him throughout his life and finally brought about his death.

RK4907
MAY 1990

The Defence of Calais, 1940.

2nd Bn The King's Royal Rifle Corps, 1st Bn The Rifle Brigade and 1st Bn The Queen Victoria's Rifles.

Churchill said of this heroic stand: "Calais was the crux. Many other causes might have prevented the deliverance of Dunkirk, but it is certain that the three days gained by the defence of Calais enabled the Gravelines waterline to be held, and that without this, even in spite of Hitler's vacillations and Runstedt's orders all would have been cut off and lost."

This picture, which was commissioned by the Rifle Brigade Club in 1966, shows the final phase of the action. Unfortunately as Cuneo was about to set off for Calais he discovered that passports don't last for ever:

"The very morning the Regiment had arranged to fly me over to France in a light aircraft, I discovered my passport had expired! However on landing in Calais it was explained to a sympathetic official that 'Colonel' Cuneo's absent-mindedness was a by-word with the Regiment, and all was forgiven. Then, in company with my friend David Stileman (now Brigadier) and one other officer who had been through the action, we retraced the whole thing, step by step, from Calais Ville to the port. It was only when I clambered on to the last remaining German bunker between the station and the sea, that I knew we had found the perfect location for the picture."

Making sketches for the 7 foot canvas of the 'Defence of Calais', for the Royal Green Jackets.

The Ringed Wellington. April 1940.

This somewhat unorthodox Wellington bomber, code-named 'Directional Wireless Installation' or 'DWI' for short was a highly successful answer to a serious problem in World War II. The amount of shipping being lost through the indiscriminate sowing of magnetic mines had reached 'war-loss' proportions. In DWI a powerful motor generator was installed in the aircraft fuselage. This supplied a heavy current to a large coil carried in the circular casing.
The resulting magnetic field triggered off the mechanism in the mine causing it to explode. There is no doubt that this brilliant concept saved many Allied ships from a watery grave.

The first test of DWI was over the Thames estuary and the pilot was told to go no lower than 50 feet. He kept going lower and lower until a mine went off neatly detaching his tailplane. When the procedure became routine the operating height was about 100 feet - low enough! Throughout the time the prototype was being put together, Churchill (then First Lord of the Admiralty) insisted that a set of photographs be sent to him each night to show how much progress had been made in the previous 24 hours. Sir George Edwards, who directed the project, says he never worked under harder pressure than on that job – but he understood the necessity when he read Gilbey's biography of Churchill covering that period.

The last time the Wellingtons were used was sweeping the Suez Canal.

CUNEO
AUGUST 1944

The Battle of Sidi Saleh

Western Desert, February 1941

Early February 1941 saw the 7th Armoured Division in hot pursuit of the Italian 10th Army in the approaches to Derna. On 3 February they paused for rest and for ammunition to be brought forward. Then came news that the enemy were moving out of Benghazi and seemed set to retreat from Cyrenaica completely. There was no time for rest. An armoured force was despatched to move at speed across 150 miles of desert to cut the Benghazi – Tripoli road, along which the Italians would be moving. 2nd Battalion Rifle Brigade was to take part in the chase.

By 14.00 hours on 5 February a company of the Rifle Brigade was in position across the road at Sidi Saleh, with C Squadron, 11th Hussars on their right. Two more companies were in the rear protecting the gun postions of the Royal Horse Artillery. Within half-an-hour of the infantry arriving, the leading column of the Italian 10th Army was seen approaching. The ensuing action was short but fierce. The Hussars knocked out the escorting enemy tanks, while the Rifle Brigade brought accurate and intense rifle and Bren-gun fire to bear on the 'soft-skinned' vehicles and their occupants. Suddenly, and to their surprise, the RHA found some 200 Italians approaching the gun positions asking to surrender.

Just after 17.00 hours a much larger enemy column came into view. There were signs that the enemy were bringing their artillery forward. Seeing the danger to his exposed left flank, the commanding officer of the Rifle Brigade closed the gap with two more companies. The fighting was hard. The RHA continued to bombard the oncoming vehicles and artillery. At 18.00 hours units of the British 4th Armoured Brigade fell on the rear of the enemy column. At the sight of more British armour the enemy seemed to lose all will to fight and searched for anyone who would take them prisoner. At the end of the day the reserve company of 2nd Bn Rifle Brigade were holding 5,000 Italians prisoner.

Test Pilot.

29 January 1940.
Sketch made by Cuneo
in the air of a Ghost
Lancastrian on test.

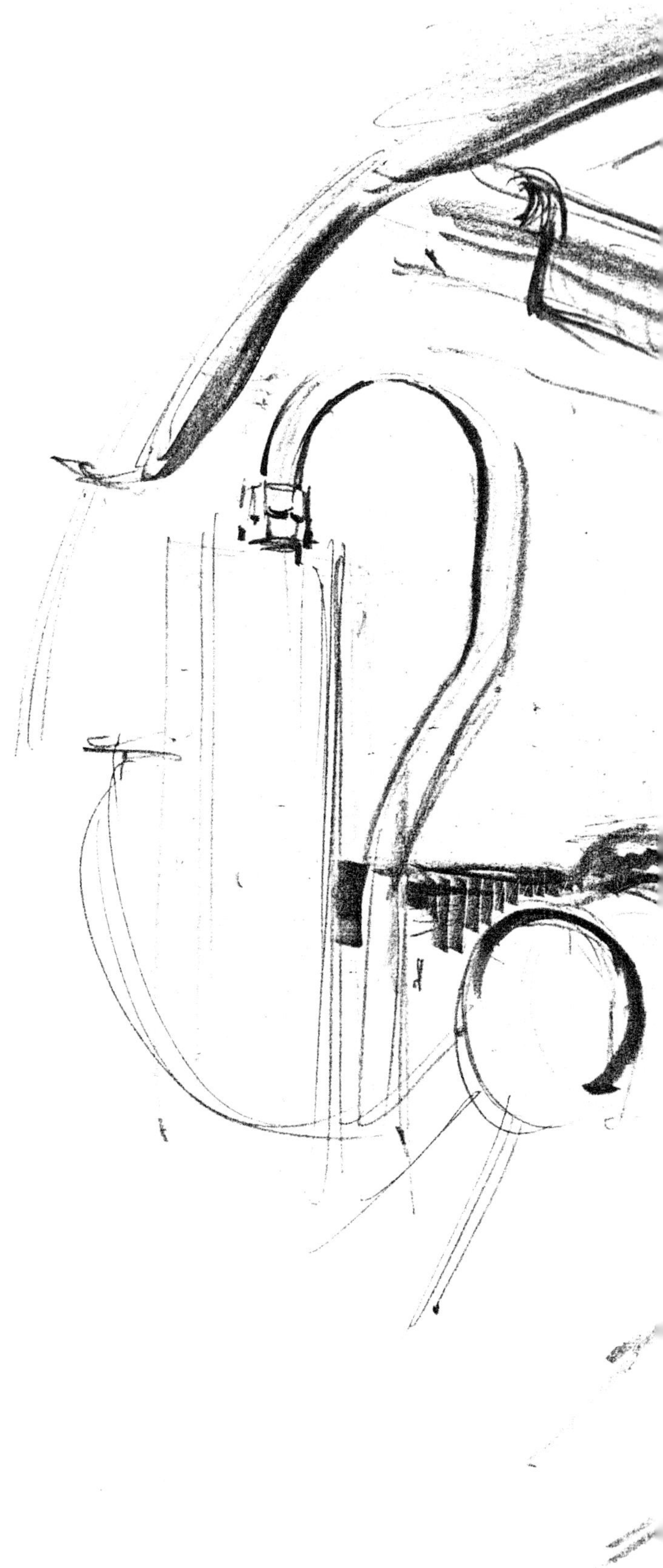

Cockpit view
of Ghost Lancastrian.
29/1/48

The Battle of Sidi Rezegh

21 November 1941.

This painting was commissioned by Martin Farndale when commanding 7th Armoured Brigade, the Desert Rats, in 1972. It depicts the last battle the brigade fought in the Western Desert when it was all but wiped out at Sidi Rezegh, in what is now Libya, in November 1941.

The Commander-in-Chief, General Auchinleck, was determined to chase Rommel out of Cyrenaica, the eastern province of Libya, and relieve Tobruk. As part of this battle 7th Armoured Brigade attacked Sidi Rezegh airfield and was in turn attacked itself on 21 November 1941 by 21st Panzer Division. Five survivors of the battle, including George Davy, the Brigade Commander, seen in this picture in his 11th Hussars side hat in the top of his tank, and Noel Wall, his Brigade Major, running towards him, met several times to supervise the painting of their battle. They made many corrections and Cuneo showed great forbearance throughout - but the end result is very authentic. They all remembered the black smoke and the Battery Commander of F Battery RHA coolly directing fire from his 'soft-skinned' 15 cwt truck.

The painting shows the moment when the 7th Hussars, to the left of centre, took the full shock of the German attack and were severely mauled, while the 2nd Royal Tanks attacked from the right with 50 tanks. That night the Brigade was no more and the remnants went to Cairo to refit. It was next sent to Burma and then to Syria and Italy before returning to England in time for the D-Day landings. It fought across Europe and ended the War in Berlin. A magnificent record. But it never fought harder than it did at Sidi Rezegh, as shown in this splendid painting.

The Battle of Knightsbridge, 6 June 1942.

Western Desert (Cyrenaica).

Names familiar to the British 8th Army, eg Knightsbridge, were often used to identify key points in largely unmapped and featureless desert. The Battle of 'Knightsbridge' was part of the Battle of the Cauldron fought by the 8th Army in the Western Desert between 2 - 11 June 1942. After days of fierce fighting, tanks of Rommel's Afrika Corps broke into the British positions and forced the 8th Army to withdraw to Alamein. Very large numbers of tanks and guns were lost.

The picture shows the scene at the Cauldron, three and a half miles west of 'Knightsbridge' where on 6 June, 426th Battery of 107 Regt Royal Horse Artillery (The South Nottinghamshire Hussars) made their gallant last stand as enemy tanks attacked them for three days. In the end they were engaging the enemy at point-blank range. With all ammunition gone, and having suffered severe casualties, those who remained – almost every one of them wounded – were forced to surrender. Their Regimental History records "Right well had the South Notts Hussars carried out their orders to stand and fight to the last man and the last round."

Great gallantry was shown that day as the Gunners fought around their colours – the guns. 307th Battery (The South Notts Hussars) is still part of the Army – in 100th Regiment RA (TA). It has never forgotten the bravery of its forbears and celebrates the anniversary of this Battle every year.

TERENCE · CUNEO ·
SEPTEMBER
1978

Breaching the Minefields. El Alamein. October 1942.

The Royal Engineers opening the way through the enemy minefields for the armour of the 8th Army to break through at the Battle of Alamein on the night of 23 October 1942.

"To stand erect. To walk slowly. To listen for the warning shriek in a headset. To gently, so gently, probe beneath the ground and lift death from the soil. To be unhurried, meticulous and yet to remain detached from a surrounding, veritable hell. Here is bravery!"

CUNEO
FEBRUARY 1950

The 'Snipe' or Kidney Ridge Action

El Alamein, 27 October 1942, The 2nd Battalion, The Rifle Brigade.

This is the Commanding Officer's own description of the event:

"At 13.00 hours nine tanks attacked our south-west flank. Only Sgt Calistan's gun was able to bear. I made Calistan hold his fire till the leading tank was 600 yards off. Then he did some wonderful shooting, brewing up six, one after the other. The remaining three tanks kept coming on, blazing away with their MGs. Calistan was now almost out of ammunition, so Lieut Jack Toms, his platoon Commander, brought up some in a jeep, but the jeep was hit and set on fire about 10 yards behind the gun. We managed however to manhandle the ammunition to the gun and with the next three shots Calistan scored a hat-trick accounting for the remaining three tanks."

Lieutenant Colonel V. B. Turner was awarded the Victoria Cross for the part he played in the 'Snipe' action.

This painting was the first battle subject Cuneo ever did for the army. He started by getting individual accounts of the action from the three survivors. Colonel Turner was the first to arrive at Cuneo's studio. He described his recollection of the events, adding:

"It was a dull day. Very overcast. In fact it was damned chilly and I wasn't sorry to be wearing this thing." He showed Cuneo the jerkin he had brought along, the stains of dried blood still visible on the leather. The next day Jack Toms and the Corporal who had helped recover the ammunition gave their stories, how the jeep was 'brewed up' as the Colonel snatched the last ammo box from the bonnet, how Turner was hit in the head a second later. All in all, their reports were identical with Colonel Turner's - except for *one* detail. They were both adamant that the day was blazing hot and they were all fighting under a *scorching* noonday sun!

·CUNEO·
JUNE 1951

Major H. W. (Pat) Le Patourel, VC

2nd Battalion The Hampshire Regiment.
Tebourba Gap, Tunisia, North Africa, 3 December 1942.

The Hampshires had been locked in combat with the German paratroopers for three days. At 11.00 hours on the fourth day the enemy launched an attack on all the positions still held by the now depleted 2nd Battatlion, concentrating their heaviest fire on the Battalion's left flank. After about an hour the Germans had secured the high ground and brought heavy machine-gun fire to bear. The situation looked hopeless. Major Le Patourel decided to launch one last desperate attack to clear the enemy from their commanding position.
His brave action was to win him the Victoria Cross.
The citation read:

"This officer personally led four volunteers under very heavy fire to the top in a last attempt to dislodge several enemy machine-guns. The party was heavily engaged by machine-gun fire and Major Le Patourel rallied his men several times and engaged the enemy silencing several machine-gun posts. Finally, when the remainder of his party were all killed or wounded, he went forward alone with a pistol and some grenades to attack enemy machine-guns at close quarters, and from this action he did not return.
Major Le Patourel's most gallant conduct and self-sacrifice, his brilliant leadership and tenacious devotion to duty in the face of a determined enemy were beyond praise."

It was believed that Le Patourel had been killed, and indeed, his Victoria Cross was awarded 'posthumously'. Later it was discovered that he had been seriously wounded and taken prisoner.

Brownings on Test, 1942.

The chattering roar of four Browning machine guns firing in unison, is, to say the least - noisy! Cuneo had to make this drawing barely six feet from their muzzles. He was, of course, wearing ear-muffs but even with this protection the din was fearsome.

The guns were fired in 20-round bursts, each burst being punctuated by the inclusion of one dummy round, before firing is able to recommence once more. At the end, Cuneo was more than happy to leave the place.

CUNEO
JAN 1945

The Last Halifax

In April 1942 the German battleship 'Tirpitz', a formidable and persistent threat to Allied shipping in the Atlantic, was sighted lying at anchor in a fjord near Trondheim in Norway. The Royal Air Force was ordered to attack and sink her. Swiftly and in great secrecy Nos. 10, 35 and 76 Squadrons, equipped with Halifax bombers, were brought together at Kinloss in Scotland and made ready for their daunting task. Its enormous importance to the war effort was stressed in messages to the RAF from Prime Minister Churchill who referred to the mission as "something you will be proud to relate to your grandchildren."

At 20.30 hours on 27 April the squadrons took off. No. 76 Squadron was to attack from about 4,000 feet using 4,000-pound bombs. Nos. 10 and 35 Squadrons, each aeroplane carrying four 'sea-mine' bombs, were to follow, coming in low and making their final approach at deck-height. One of the 11 Halifaxes of 35 Squadron was a brand-new aircraft on its first operational sortie. Its number was S-W1046 ('S-Sugar'). It was destined to be 'The Last Halifax'.

S-Sugar arrived at the target and flying low between the hills on either side of the fjord moved down towards the German dreadnought. Suddenly the crew found themselves in a terrifying hail of gunfire. It was the heaviest flak they had ever faced and seemed to be coming from every direction at once. The Tirpitz put up smoke so dense that the pilot could not see his instruments and was forced to pull off the hatch blind and but for his navigator's warning would have crashed into the hills on the right of the fjord. The bombs were released but it was impossible to see their effect. About three minutes later S-Sugar was hit. Smoke and flame belched from the starboard wing and outer engine and it was obvious she was never going to make it back to England. The pilot could not gain height and looked desperately for somewhere to put down. He spotted a nearby lake which he thought should be frozen, but frozen or not he had to go for it. He nursed S-Sugar down. The lake was indeed frozen and the hapless plane slithered to a halt, the starboard wing still ablaze and behind it a flare path of fire as spilled gasolene ignited. All six members of the crew jumped clear. In due course, five of them got back to England through neutral Sweden, one was injured and remained a prisoner of the Germans until the war ended. The aircraft sank.

S-W1048 remained at the bottom of Lake Hoklingen until June 1973 when it was recovered by an RAF team. It was then the last-known Halifax in existence. Despite having been submerged for over 30 years its was in remarkable condition and when a new battery was fitted the cockpit lights came on! S-Sugar was lovingly restored and is now at the Royal Air Force Museum at Hendon.

Although severely damaged, Tirpitz survived the raid. On the 19 November 1944 she was attacked by a force of 32 Lancaster bombers and finally crippled beyond repair.

Captain The Lord Lyell, VC

The action at Djebel Bou Aoukaz, Tunisia – 27 April 1943

The beginning of 1943 found Rommel trapped between the pursuing 8th Army and the Anglo-American force under General Eisenhower which had landed in French North-Africa. Although he was still able to deal some sharp blows to the Americans in the region of the Kasserine Pass, Tunisia, his time was running out. The action at Djebel Bou Aoukaz that Cuneo has depicted took place less than three weeks before the Axis forces in Tunisia laid down their arms.

The only living witness to this carnage was the corporal who supported Lyell and who can be seen lying prone in the distance firing down into the 88 mm gun position, which 1st Battalion, Scots Guards, were determined to take. The other supporting Scotsman was killed outright, leaving Lyell to charge the site single-handed. With pistol in one hand and dirk in the other, the intrepid 22-year old leapt forward firing and slashing at the enemy. Five men fell at his hand, before he was finally overpowered and hacked to death within yards of the gun he had given his life to silence. Captain The Lord Lyell won the posthumous award of the Victoria Cross. Corporal J. R. Lawrie and Guardsman J. Chisholm were each awarded the Military Medal.

Intelligence Corps. 'Operation Bodyline'

The photographic interpretation operation that helped Bomber command destroy the VI sites. Medmenham, Bucks. December 1943 - July 1944.

The Army Photographic Interpretation Section became B Section of the newly formed Central Interpretation Unit in October 1940 and was charged with the study of German ground defences and artillery sites in occupied Europe.

In 1943 the Section was ordered to watch especially for new design, long-range artillery likely to be used to bombard England. It was suspected that rocket research was going on at Peenemunde and that a new weapon, capable of being fired from a long tube, was being developed. Although no trace of such a system could be found, the photographic interpreters (PIs) did locate a number of unusual constuction sites in the Pas de Calais area. Some 70 locations were plotted, each having two blockhouse buildings, a curving 'ski-type' blast wall and a ramp. The PIs analysis was put to the Air Ministry but the suggestion that the sites could be used to launch some new type of aircraft was dismissed. However, on 25th November 1943, on a test ramp at Peenemunde, the first sighting was made of a 'flying bomb' - the V1. It was obvious that the construction sites discovered by B Section were designed to launch this deadly weapon. The Air Ministry was notified at once and the Cabinet was briefed. As a result, 'Operation Bodyline' was initiated and a special section set up to intensify the search for V1 sites. Within ten days, 96 sites had been identified and Bomber Command was ordered to destroy them; before the end of the year, 92 had been eliminated. Then, in April 1944, B Section identified the first of a series of new, modified sites in Northern France. Although virtually all interpretation resources were now concentrated on D Day preparations, the Section still managed to locate 67 new flying bomb sites and on 1 June the Air Ministry was warned that they were operational. 34 hours later the first V1 landed on London. Bomber Command made further strikes but the needs of the Normandy invasion precluded complete destruction of all the new sites and 45 of them were still operational in mid-June. By the end of June some 2,000 V1s had been launched against London and the South-east of England.

B section's belief that the actual missiles were not kept at the launching sites but in the Neucourt caves, in the Somme area, was proved correct when, in July, following movement in that region, a total of 106 V1s were launched. B Section requested a Bomber Command raid on Neucourt. The raid was successful and thereafter no V1s were launched from the Somme area.

Cuneo's painting shows members of B Section plotting V1 sites in December 1943. The contribution this small unit, less than 30 all ranks, made to the destruction of the flying bomb sites was, by any measure, outstanding.

Keep mum
she's not so dumb!
CLASS
WASTE

Shoes for Bombers

Moulding the great tyres for Lancaster aircraft. A seemingly humdrum but vital part of the famous bomber.

The Lancaster was perhaps the most famous, and certainly the most successful, heavy bomber used by the Royal Air Force in World War II. By March 1945 there were 56 squadrons of Lancasters (745 aircraft) in first line service with Bomber Command. During the War they flew a total of 156,000 sorties and dropped 608,612 tons of bombs. An outstanding feature of the Lancaster was its ability to carry bombs of ever-increasing size. Originally designed to carry 4,000-pound bombs, it went on to carry 12,000-pounders; then the 12,000-pound deep-penetration 'Tallboy', and finally the 22,000-pound 'Grand Slam'. There were many daring Lancaster raids. Two that caught the headlines were the attack on the Mohne and Eder dams in Germany by 617 Squadron (the Dambusters) in May 1943, and the sinking of the German battleship 'Tirpitz' in a Norwegian fjord in November 1944 by 18 Lancasters of No.617 Squadron and 13 of No. 9 Squadron. Heading a long list of awards for gallantry to captains and crews of the Lancasters were no less than 10 Victoria Crosses.

·CUNEO·
·NOV·1945·

Amazon Bridge over the Rapido River

4th Divisional Engineers building the Amazon Bridge over the Rapido River, near Monte Cassino, Italy. 12-13 May 1944.

Cuneo recalls:

"For this painting of the crossing of the Rapido, the Royal Engineers agreed to build a full scale Bailey bridge which I could use as a model for my studies. However, on arriving at Aldershot, I found to my consternation that I was looking at the most immaculate structure imaginable. The thing had naturally been assembled with absolute precision, but it was spotlessly clean, the decking looked scrubbed and there was a railed footwalk either side.'I'm afraid this won't do', I said. 'I must have something much more rugged, something that has obviously been assembled in haste and under pressure – perhaps only half-decked and weighted at one end to give a cantilever effect.' The point was noted and without fuss or comment the 'showroom' bridge was dismantled and exactly the sort of thing I had in mind rapidly erected in its place. The Sappers then laid on a squad of men who, at my instruction, took up poses of pushing and straining at the metal sections. I was put in the bucket of a great mechanical shovel and hoisted 15 feet in the air. From this exalted viewpoint I made my drawings.

"It was only in the studio later that a quiet morning's work at Aldershot was transformed into the violent nightmare scene that the real thing must have been. As always, the Sappers at Aldershot were patient and understanding, doing everything I asked with good humour – although I sensed a slight touch of injured pride at the suggestion that any bridge built by the RE under fire in battle would be anything less than a superb piece of work!"

Scots Guards in the Bocage

Action of the Right Flank, 3rd Bn Scots Guards during the advance from Caumont to Les Loges, Normandy, 30 July 1944.

Owing to their length and weight of tracks, the Churchills were the only tanks capable of surmounting the exceptionally high banks in the Bocage without turning over backwards – to the astonishment of the Germans. The commander of 'Lochinvar' survived to become Bishop of St Albans and later Archbishop of Canterbury. He also won the Military Cross. At the time he was Lieutenant Robert Runcie.

Attack on Gestapo Headquarters

24 April 1944.

Group Captain Leonard (later Lord) Cheshire, VC, DSO, DFC, piloting a Mosquito Mark VI, drops markers on the Gestapo Headquarters in Munich, thus setting out the target for the waiting bombers overhead.

During the course of the work, Cuneo met Leonard Cheshire: "He visited my studio on several occasions during the construction of this painting and gave me a graphic idea of what that night was like. The defences of Munich were of course elaborate and flak and tracer made the enterprise a veritable nightmare. His job was to fly in low, drop the red markers and climb to safety with all the speed his two Merlins could give him. Cool courage if ever there was.

"At home I am proud to have a framed print of this painting bearing Cheshire's autograph. He wrote 'To Terence Cuneo, in admiration of a skilful and beautiful work of art - and with happy memories of working with him. Leonard Cheshire.' I treasure that print."

The Battle of Cassino, Italy. May 1944.

This depicts the 8th Army artillery firing at night in the fourth and final Battle of Cassino in May 1944. The army artillery, comprising over 600 guns destroyed the last remaining German defences centred on the monastery which was the linchpin of the Gustav Line, south of Rome. The painting shows medium guns – 5.5-inch – in action. The artillery of 10th and 13th British, 1st Canadian and 2nd Polish Corps fought the battle of Cassino, together with those of the 2nd, 6th, 1st Canadian and 2nd Polish Army Groups, Royal and Polish Artilleries. It was a massive fire plan.

Cuneo's own account of working on this painting reveals much about his integrity concerning technical aspects:

"To me the old 5.5 was a gun that looked like a gun, a truly terrific piece of field artillery. I made a trip down to Warminster to see this gun at work and I took Andrew, my grandson, along with me. With plugs of wax stuffed into our ears, we witnessed the gun fire round after round and watched the shells bursting in the distance. Andrew was enthralled, but was made to stand some way back. I had to be much nearer – within seven or eight feet of the breech – to get a true feeling of the gun's behaviour and to observe and take notes of all that went on – the shell being lifted from its cradle, the breech action, the flash from the muzzle, the recoil, the reloading and sighting of the gun and, above all, the actions of the crew. These things cannot be faked in a picture; they have to be seen actually happening if one is to achieve authenticity. I remember once seeing an illustration depicting a heavy gun in action. The artist had really gone to town on the fiery flash from the barrel, but unfortunately he had painted the breech *still open*! You can imagine this rather original approach astonished some Gunner friends!"

Mosquitos on the line at Hatfield, 1944.

One of a series of paintings Cuneo did for de Havillands depicting every stage of Mosquito construction. It was fascinating seeing how that incredible wooden aeroplane was put together, much of it incidentally in High Wycombe furniture factories. It was here at Hatfield, whilst working on this particular painting that Cuneo first met Frank Wootton, the celebrated aircraft painter. He remembers that Frank gave him a useful tip concerning a detail on his half-finished painting. Happily, since then their paths have continued to cross from time to time.

Lance-Sergeant J. D. Baskeyfield, VC

2nd Battalion The South Staffordshire Regiment
(The Prince of Wales's). Arnhem, 1944.

On 20 September 1944 during the battle at Arnhem, Holland, Lance-Sergeant J. D. Baskeyfield was in charge of a 6-pounder anti-tank gun. In the course of the engagement, when two Tiger tanks and at least one self-propelled gun were destroyed, all his crew became casualties and he himself was severely wounded. Quite alone, he continued to man the gun, keeping the enemy at bay, until it was put out of action.

Dragging a shattered leg, he crawled across the road to the firing position of an undamaged 6-pounder, whose crew had been killed, and proceeded to man it single-handed. He fired two shots, one of which knocked out an advancing self-propelled gun, and was preparing to fire again when, seconds after the scene Cuneo has shown, he was killed. The Victoria Cross was awarded posthumously. He was 21 years old.

TERENCE · CUNEO ·
JUNE 1970 ·

Captain T. R. Galloway, MC

Intelligence Corps. Europe 1944.

In September 1944 during the campaign in North-west Europe a forward British battalion brought in three civilians for questioning. They were interrogated by Captain Galloway who found they were not civilians but German soldiers of the Brandenburg Division who had been sent across the River Maas on a special mission and who were due to return across the river by boat the same night. Having discovered the location of the rendezvous, Galloway decided to go to it himelf and give the signal to bring the enemy boat to the British bank. An ambush was laid and at the appointed time he stood up striking matches in his cupped hands (the agreed signal). He presented a clear target as he stood in full view on the moonlit bank. His signal was acknowledged and a boat put out. When it beached Galloway called, in German, for the occupants to come ashore and help him with a wounded comrade. As they landed he drew his pistol and ordered them to put their hands up and throw down the weapons with which they were covering him. Firing broke out at once from the boat and from two Spandau machine-guns across the river. Our own guns covering the ambush replied. The Germans who had landed dashed for the boat but Galloway, regardless of the hail of fire from both banks, fired at the enemy, hitting one with a pistol shot. The boat pushed off from the bank but was at once riddled by machine-gun fire and was last seen sinking in mid-stream. It appeared that none of the occupants reached their own bank.

Cuneo has depicted this brave officer standing alone and firing at the enemy. He was awarded the Military Cross.

Crossing the Indaw Chaung River

Burma. 1944

The Chindit campaign of 1944 took place in the mountainous jungles of northern Burma far behind the Japanese lines. This painting portrays a day in the five-month campaign when the Ist Bn The Bedfordshire and Hertfordshire Regiment was crossing a river in the jungle.

In the foreground, with arm outstretched, Lt.-Col T. J. Barrow issues orders to one of his Column Commanders. To the right the radio operator is making morse contact with base 250 miles away in India. The pack mules are loaded with reserve ammunition, Vickers machine-guns, flame-throwers, petrol and medical stores. Each man carries some 70 lbs of kit. The elephants, used for carrying the wounded and stores, were hired locally and paid for in silver and opium. The lone donkey carried a Column Commander's kit and stores (this much loved creature was the only animal to complete the whole of the fearsome Chindit campaign and was eventually flown back to India; nice to know the 'old soldier' survived the ordeal). Not shown in the picture are the four oxen, supplied as meat on the hoof. The American light aircraft in the background is being loaded with seriously wounded. More sick and wounded are about to be taken downstream to Kamaing. Fires burn as a result of Japanese shelling. On the far bank the small whitewashed pagoda is guarded by a stone Chinthe, the mythical animal, half-lion, half-eagle, which became the Chindit symbol.

CUNEO
OCTOBER 1989

The Battle of Kohima. April 1944.

This painting was commissioned by Martin Farndale when he was commanding 2nd Armoured Division. It depicts the Division's great battle in Burma at Kohima in 1944. The Japanese 31st Division spearheaded the attack to break over the mountains of north-west Burma and into India. At Kohima in their path stood 2nd Division. The battle lasted four weeks and was vicious, close-quarter, hand-to-hand combat. The crisis came when the Japanese reached the tennis court by the District Commissioner's bungalow, the ruins of which can be seen on the right of the painting. The time came to eject them. The Engineers winched a Grant tank up to the British end of the tennis court; the Japanese were dug in at the other end. On the left of the painting can be seen one of the two 3.7-inch mountain guns that were brought into action. Centrally, the painting shows the tank escorting the lead platoon of 2nd Dorsets across the tennis court and ejecting the Japanese. In this bitter action, fought in a stench of rotting bodies, the only way to get at some of the enemy was to winkle them out of their foxholes with delay-fused grenades mounted on long bamboo poles. In the centre of the picture two of the Dorsets can be seen administering this lethal treatment.

Victory soon came. Like Alamein in the Western Desert, Kohima was a turning point in the War and the Division went on to Mandalay and Rangoon.

Every year some 300 old Comrades hold a Service of Remembrance at their memorial in York, a replica of the one left at the tennis court, on which are inscribed the words:

"When you go home,
Tell them of us and say
For their tomorrow
We gave our today."

D-Day, Normandy, 6 June 1944.

Cuneo painted this picture to mark the 40th anniversary of D-Day when the Allied armies landed on the beaches of Normandy to complete the task of defeating the German army in the field. The picture raised a great deal of money through its sale and the sale of reproductions, all of which was used to relieve suffering amongst soldiers and their dependants. The story of how the painting was done is told on pages 27–28.

LcT709
LcA671

Pioneers, Sword Beach, D-Day, Normandy

To mark the occasion of the disbandment of the Royal Pioneer Corps, Cuneo was commissioned to portray the activities of the Pioneers during the D-Day landings, when probably the greatest ever concentration of Pioneers on operations was recorded.

Pioneers were among the first British troops to land on the beaches of Normandy on D-Day, as part of Operation Overlord on 6 June 1944. The build up of the force was very rapid, and by D+25 all the Pioneer units allotted to the Second Army, amounting to 14 Pioneer Group Headquarters and 115 Companies (35,500 men) were in Normandy.

CUNEO
FEBRUARY '93

The Crossing of the Rhine

44th Bn The Royal Tank Regiment, 4th Armoured Brigade,
24 March 1945.

It is quite unbelievable that these primitive toy-like canvas boats could be successful in floating Sherman Tanks across a river. But they were. A piece of invention that beggars belief.

Private James Stokes, The King's Shropshire Light Infantry, winning the VC at Kervenheim, 1 March 1945.

On 1 March 1945, 2nd Battalion The King's Shropshire Light Infantry launched an attack on an enemy postion in the village of Kervenheim, Rhineland. In support were tanks of No. 2 Squadron, 4th Battalion Coldstream Guards. The German position, in a group of farm buildings, was strongly defended by parachute troops equipped with Spandau machine-guns. Despite harassing fire from the tanks, the Germans held their ground, moving quickly between buildings as the British fire switched from target to target. The going was bad and the tanks could not keep up with the infantry who were themselves under heavy fire from both flanks. The platoon of which Private James Stokes was a member was pinned down by intense rifle and machine-gun fire from a farm building. Stokes dashed into the building, firing from the hip and reappeared with 12 prisoners. During the operation he was wounded but refused to go to the Regimental Aid Post to have his wounds dressed, remaining with his platoon to continue the advance. He rushed another house, taking five more prisoners. By this time he was suffering severely from his injuries but insisted on taking part in the bayonet attack on the final objective. Only 20 yards from the enemy position he fell, mortally wounded. His outstanding bravery in the face of the enemy was recognised by the posthumous award of the Victoria Cross.

In 1963 The King's Shropshire Light Infantry commissioned Cuneo to paint a commemorative picture of Stokes' gallant action. Having studied the record of the encounter with great care, Cuneo visited Kervenheim to go over the ground. In the village chemist's he was shown a photograph, said to have been taken soon after the action, of 'Lion', the tank of a troop commander from No. 2 Squadron - Captain Alec Foucard. The tank appeared to be close to the position of the infantry's final assault. He completed his picture, giving, quite properly, pride of place to James Stokes but also showing Foucard's tank well up. When the picture was seen by General Sir Geoffrey Musson, Colonel of the Regiment, he expressed concern that all was not right. He described the position of the tank as wrong and a 'military nonsense' which, if left uncorrected, could only cast doubt on Stokes' action. Cuneo was asked to paint out the tank and, with some misgivings in view of the photograph he had seen, did so. His action stirred a hornet's nest. The tank commander protested; the company commander of the infantry expressed surprise and the Tank Squadron Commander was 'distressed'. Cuneo began to wish he had never altered the painting. The Coldstream felt the omission of the tank devalued their part in the action, which had been warmly praised at the time, especially by the infantry company commander, and for which Captain Foucard was awarded the Military Cross.

On deeper reflection, and with the help of a letter from Lieutenant Banks who commanded Stokes' platoon, a number of points became clear. First, the tank 'Lion', while making an enormous contribution to the success of the action, was not able to fire during the final assault since its HE shells were instantaneous-fuzed and fired on the enemy at such short range would have endangered our own troops. Second, the photograph seen by Cuneo had been taken on the 2nd March when 'Lion' went forward to help in consolidating the position – and silencing the remaining Spandau machine-gun. Finally, Banks averred that his recollection of the facts was "as clear as if the action took place yesterday" and that the support given by the tank troop was 'superb'. So, all in all, the prime object of the painting – depicting Stokes' deed of great valour – was best achieved by omitting the tank from the picture of the brave infantry charge on 1 March 1945.

The German Surrender at Lüneburg Heath

May 1945.

A pity it never occurred to anyone at the time that an artist (preferably Cuneo!) should be present to record this historic scene. This interpretation, commissioned after the war, was of necessity based partly on a black and white photograph and partly on the Field Marshal's own recollection. Both were a little hazy. (See pages 24–25).

The King's Dinner, Woolwich.

This dinner was held at Woolwich on 4 December 1950, St Barbara's Day (the Patron Saint of all Gunners). King George VI is clearly seen at the head of the table with the Master Gunner, Field Marshal Viscount Alanbrooke, sitting beside him. It was at this dinner that the King expressed his wish to become 'Captain-General' to the Royal Regiment of Artillery instead of 'Colonel in Chief' as all monarchs had been since 1722. To this day the Loyal Toast in the Royal Regiment is 'The Queen – our Captain-General'. The Mess Room is the oldest in the British Army, unaltered (except for decoration) since it was built in 1781. On special occasions the Mess staff wear their 18th Century dress and wigs, as depicted.

The Royal Artillery Orchestra in the foreground, is the oldest orchestra of any kind, military or civilian in Britain. On this occasion they played under the baton of their famous Director of Music, Lieutenant-Colonel Geary. Some of the fabulous silver of Woolwich is on display. Special dinners of this sort are still held in the Mess from time to time. Her Majesty Queen Elizabeth II has dined there with her officers on two occasions.

But it is not all pomp and circumstance. At 07.00 hours, or earlier, officers in working dress can be seen taking breakfast at these same tables at the start of the working day.

Cuneo has vivid recollections of a discussion with Lord Alanbrooke about this picture. (See page 22).

First presentation of colours

1st, 2nd and 3rd Battalions, The Parachute Regiment
by King George VI. Aldershot, July 1950.

This picture marks the beginning of Cuneo's long and happy association with the Army. It was not without its difficulties but Field Marshal Montgomery was on hand to give advice. The full story is on page 20.

The Assault at Imjin River

Korea. St George's Day, 23 April 1951.

This dawn scene shows 25 pounders firing in support of Infantry of the Royal Northumberland Fusiliers on the heights north of the river. Some guns firing over open sights at the Chinese infiltrating across the Imjin. Note that the officer is wearing a rose in his cap, specially flown in from Japan for the celebration of St George's Day.

Hook Action, Korea. 1953.

The trouble to which the Royal Engineers went to stage this night scene from the Korean War, was just about the most elaborate the Army ever put on for an artist. On the night chosen, two 3-tonners plus a couple of staff cars and a Land Rover drove on to the sand pit of Oxshott heath and began unloading men, equipment, floodlights and generators, rolls of concertina wire, slabs of concrete and an assortment of tools, picks and shovels and heaven knows what else.
By this time it was pitch dark. The floodlights were now turned on, the generators roared and by the time everything was set up and models were posed all over the sandpit, the thing looked more like something out of a Cecil B. de Mille extravaganza than a lot of soldiers trying to help an artist prepare his picture!

For good measure, flares were periodically shot into the sky, producing an eerie effect. It was really quite something! Cuneo worked like a beaver for a full two hours or more, making notes and generally absorbing the atmosphere.

Presentation of the new Standard

to the 4th/7th Royal Dragoon Guards, Fallingbostel, Germany, 23 May 1958.

Cuneo recalls: "I well remember when Field Marshal Sir Gerald Templer came to my studio to pose for this picture. Having studied himself in my long mirror to check the correctness of his uniform, he approached me. Placing his face about 18 inches away from my own he treated me to a hard stare. 'I don't mind what the devil you make of my face, Cuneo, but for God's sake get the uniform right!'. . . I like to think I did."

TERENCE CUNEO
NOVEMBER 1958

The Queen's visit

to the Staff College, Camberley, 1958.

Candidates for entry to the Staff College, Camberley are required to pass an entrance examination and to be recommended for staff training. Although an officer's further advancement in his career is not dependant on being staff-trained, it is rare for the highest ranks in the Army to be attained without having successfully completed the course at Camberley.

Cuneo remembers: "They built me an elevated platform from which to portray this scene and almost sthe entire work was completed on the spot, in paint. The line of officers in the foreground all posed individually including the Commandant. Her Majesty and the Duke of Edinburgh graciously gave sittings at the Palace. The Commandant told me after the ceremony, that when the Queen entered the hall and saw me up there on my platform, she smiled and said to the Commandant, 'Every time I see Mr Cuneo, he seems to be up in the air.' "

TERENCE CUNEO
SEPTEMBER 1958

Ceremony in a Chapel

His Majesty King Olav V of Norway, Colonel-in-Chief, The Green Howards, unveiling the memorial to his father His Late Majesty King Haakon VII, Colonel-in-Chief 1942-57, in the Regimental Chapel at Richmond Yorkshire, 3 June 1959.

The artist recalls: "When Archbishop Ramsey had finished posing I asked him if I might retain for a few days, his mitre, staff and cope, as I still had much detailed work to do on them. This was agreed, but now came the problem of finding a suitable person to wear them. After deliberation it was decided that the only man in the Regiment who had a figure anything like the Archbishop's was the Regimental Sergeant Major. Never will I forget seeing that stalwart pillar of military discipline robed and covered in ecclesiastical dignity, standing four square to the memorial like an avenging angel, his neck a dangerous magenta hue, the staff in his hand looking as if at any moment it might turn itself into a short Lee Enfield rifle.

Incidentally, this picture, like my Guildhall painting contains two mice. The wood-carver Thompson's in English oak climbs the rood-screen, whilst mine sits respectfully on a regimental hassock."

Final Parade of the 9th Queen's Royal Lancers

The final parade of the 9th Queen's Royal Lancers took place at Perham Down, Tidworth on 23 July 1960. Cuneo has depicted the Regiment marching past Queen Elizabeth The Queen Mother, their Colonel-in-Chief. In attendance on Her Majesty is Brigadier Christopher Peto. Leading the parade is the Commanding Officer, Lieutenant-Colonel David Lorry, riding a grey charger.

The Regiment amalgamated with the 12th Lancers to form the 9th/12th Lancers (Prince of Wales').

TERENCE CUNEO
NOVEMBER
1960

Launching Dreadnought

Britain's first nuclear-powered submarine, 'Dreadnought', was launched at Barrow shipyard on Trafalgar Day (31 October) 1960 by Her Majesty Queen Elizabeth II. She was accompanied by HRH The Duke of Edinburgh who had laid the keel of the vessel in June 1959. Cuneo recalls: "This painting was produced from a detailed drawing made on the spot. Having become accustomed to seeing, as I worked, the great sperm-whale-like creature secure on its slides, it felt strange to see it glide away into the water. I felt a sense of loss, one minute it was there and then it was gone, leaving a strange emptiness throughout the yard."

TERENCE CUNEO
JANUARY 1961

Ball given for the Queen Mother

in the Egyptian Hall of the Mansion House.
The Blues & Royals (Royal Horse Guards and First Dragoons).
November 1963.

Before the ball began Cuneo discussed with the Colonel of the Regiment the position on the floor he would like the Queen Mother to occupy amongst the other dancers in the proposed painting. He was told that his request would be put to Her Majesty but her decision could not be anticipated. It was agreed that a mark on the floor would determine the exact spot. When the Colonel raised the matter with the Queen Mother she not only complied with the request but was gracious enough to return to the spot at least six times.

Later, visiting the gallery from which Cuneo had made his sketches, the Queen Mother saw two empty champagne bottles, whereupon she turned to the Colonel and remarked: "I assume this was Mr Cuneo's inspiration".

The Chestnut Troop RHA in harbour

Germany. October 1964.

This painting was commissioned as companion to a painting already in the Troop showing it on exercise with horses in the late 19th century. The later painting was to show the Troop in 'harbour' awaiting new orders after a 'battle' in a wood in Germany. The Troop was, and still is, part of the 1st Regiment RHA and in 1964 was leaving Hildesheim for active service on the South Arabian border, north of Aden in what is now the Yemen. The picture shows, from left to right, the nose of an Austin Champ reconnaissance vehicle; the Battery Commander, Martin Farndale, giving orders at his headquarters, and a Ferret scout car from one of the Forward Observer teams. In the centre Battery Sergeant Major Pearson guides another Forward Observer tank into position; behind it is one of the huge 155-mm howitzers with which the battery was then equipped – it had six. Another is in the foreground on the right and shows the No. 1, Sergeant Brewer (Major – 1992), fitting his .5-inch machine gun while his gun detachment clean the barrel and other equipment. In the foreground Bdr Holyoake oversees the evening meal while in the distance, under camouflage netting, is a 10-ton ammunition carrier. The mouse is also present! The site is on the northern side of the Sibbesse valley, near the village of Sibbesse.

This occasion was the first meeting of Terence Cuneo and Martin Farndale and the beginning of a firm friendship. Martin recalls that, having agreed the picture should be set in the long shadows of evening, he and Terry spent several hours in a local Gasthaus waiting for the sun to set. By the time it did the outlook was very rosy indeed. When the painting was done Terry asked to drive one of the big guns (30 tons) – not an easy task even after training. However, he got in, started up and careered down a farm road with one track on top of a long row of newly-harvested potatoes – which he crushed to pulp! He made a splendid sight, crouched over the controls at top speed. It took a lot of Scotch whiskey to placate an angry farmer afterwards – but everyone was delighted with the painting which is still with the Regiment.

The Garter Ceremony. Windsor 1964.

The one person who did not pose personally for this work was Churchill. The great man, who had been made a Knight of the Garter in 1953, was unwell at the time and thus unable to attend. It was Her Majesty's wish that for posterity's sake his portrait be included. Therefore his figure had to be put in from a photograph. Churchill, whose leadership inspired the nation during World War II, was a descendant of the 1st Duke of Marlborough. He was born at Blenheim Palace in 1874 and was buried near there, at Bladon on his death in 1965.

The Lying in State of Sir Winston Churchill, KG. 25 January 1965.

Cuneo recalls:

"My only uncommissioned ceremonial painting. I awoke early on that Friday, the last day of the lying in state, with an overwhelming conviction that I must record this moment in history. I rushed to London, managed to see the Earl Marshal, and acquired a permit to enter Westminster Hall. Then off to the House of Lords to beg another permit from the Lord Great Chamberlain to enable me to draw when I got there. Having chosen my position however, the police refused to allow me to move or even to stand in front of the endless shuffling crocodile of mourners. My only hope was to sketch madly during the thirty seconds in every half-hour, when the queue was halted to enable the Watch to be changed.

"I have clear memories of the hushed, never-ending columns of figures, moving slowly past, heads turning towards the small, pathetically small in fact, draped bier raised on its dais, remote in the hollow emptiness of the hall. Somehow despite all the people, I felt curiously alone as I sketched. A week later I returned with the canvas and painted the interior of Westminster Hall direct on the spot."

The Ambush.

Operations in Borneo. 2nd Bn Royal Green Jackets – 1965.
Lt. Michael Robertson MC.

Lt. Robertson had laid his ambush only a few hundred yards from an enemy camp. He placed his riflemen close to the river; he himself, his sergeant (with a grenade launcher) and a machine gun crew, were slightly above and behind. There was no cover for any of them except when they were lying down. Seven other men of his platoon were 100 yards away covering his rear. On the third day a boat went by containing two men and equipment for many more. Soon afterwards another boat came in to the bank three yards from where Robertson and his men were concealed and remained there for some time. At 10 am a man in enemy uniform moved warily into the open on the path beyond the river followed by 11 more. The Green Jackets opened fire. Six infiltrators fell. There were 30 or 40 men behind the advance party and these quickly had two machine guns in action. Another party tried to cross the river, but withdrew when one of them was hit. Fire from the enemy guns was mostly directed at a hut in the clearing and Sergeant Hunt was able to spot both and silence them with the grenade launcher. A man who broke uphill was shot by a Section Corporal. At this point a mortar opened up from the enemy camp. Bombs fell close behind them. Robertson decided to withdraw under cover of smoke from a phosphorous grenade. "There was rather a lot of stuff flying about."

When they were safely under cover they found that a man was missing. Robertson and the sergeant went back. The man had been hit in the legs and they carried him 300 yards to where the rear party had prepared an improvised stretcher. Here Robertson called down artillery fire to cover their withdrawal, but its last stages had to be completed without support and necessitated cutting their way very slowly through a bamboo-choked ridge carrying the wounded man. 14 of the enemy had been killed or wounded. Robertson was awarded the Military Cross.

That was the report of the action but portraying the scene had its sticky moments! This painting was Cuneo's first jungle experience and he recalls that making the compositional roughs was like drawing in the hot room of a Turkish bath. His hands were wet, the pencil was wet and only by holding the sketch book well away from his body could he prevent the continuous stream of sweat from his chin from soaking the paper. He couldn't wait to get out of the almost impenetrable vegetation and back to the comparative comfort of the hot sunshine.

10th Princess Mary's Own Gurkha Rifles' first VC.

Rambahadur Limbu was serving as a lance-corporal with 10th Princess Mary's Own Gurkha Rifles on anti-terrorist operations in Sarawak. On 21 November 1965 his platoon encountered a strong enemy position on a steep hill, ahead of them and approachable only along a narrow ridge. L/Cpl Rambahadur Limbu was leading the support group in the van of the attack when they were spotted and fired on by a machine-gun, sustaining one casualty. Alone, and under intense fire, the L/Cpl stormed the enemy position and captured the machine-gun post. He redeployed his men and ran to report to his platoon commander. While he was doing this, the remainder of his group became casualties. Rambahadur Limbu returned at once, going through withering Indonesian fire to recapture the machine-gun and rescue his wounded comrades. Sadly, by the time he reached them they were already dead.

In his devotion to duty and the concern for his men Rambahadur Limbu showed complete disregard for his own safety. For this exceptional gallantry he was awarded the Victoria Cross. He continued to serve in his Regiment until he retired, as a captain, in March 1985. This painting was commissioned by his Regiment.

The Queen and the Duke of Edinburgh dining in the Mess of the Honourable Corps of Gentlemen-at-Arms

St James's Palace, 15 July 1965.

After the initial drawing, made during the dinner, each member of the Corps came to the studio for a sitting. On these occasions it was important that they should be painted wearing evening dress and this presented one irritating problem – boiled shirts! Struggling into a stiff shirt and the ensuing fight with studs and links was not popular. The problem was solved, however, by one enterprising member who arrived not with a shirt but with a waiter's 'dickey'. This, complete with collar could be attached in a moment and, when covered by a tail coat, looked surprisingly good. The collar was cut through at the back so that it could fit every neck. From then on the gallant dickey served each member of the Honourable Corps, becoming more and more dog-eared with each sitting. Nevertheless, it survived to the end, having done much to maintain Cuneo's popularity with the Gentlemen-at-Arms.

Queen Elizabeth the Queen Mother taking the Salute

at the Guidon Presentation and 250th Anniversary Parade of the 11th Hussars (Prince Albert's Own) in Hohne, Germany, 13 July 1965.

This famous cavalry regiment was raised in 1715 by King George I to protect the House of Hanover against the Stuarts. During the '45 Rebellion the Regiment took part in the Battles of Preston and later Culloden, which effectively ended the Jacobite rising.

Under the Duke of Wellington, the 11th Hussars fought in the Peninsular War against the French (1808-14) and it was during this war, according to tradition, following an action in an orchard, that they acquired the nickname 'The Cherry pickers'. At Waterloo, in 1815, they captured the last French guns in action. They were given a happy duty in 1840 when the Regiment escorted Prince Albert of Saxe-Coburg from Dover to Canterbury before his marriage to Queen Victoria. Impressed by their smartness, the Prince requested that they should thenceforth be called 'Prince Albert's Own Hussars' and should wear the crimson trousers of his livery – which they do to this day.

During the Crimean War (1835-56) the Regiment took a leading part in the heroic Charge of the Light Brigade at Balaclava, under the command of Lord Cardigan. For the remainder of the 19th century they saw service in Ireland, India, Abyssinia and South Africa.

In World War I they fought as a dismounted regiment, winning 27 battle honours. Ten years later they became the first cavalry regiment to be mechanised. They fought with great distinction during the Second World War in the Western Desert and North West Europe. The 11th Hussars amalgamated with the 10th Royal Hussars (PWO) to form the Royal Hussars (PWO) in 1969. The Royal Hussars amalgamated with the 14th/20th King's Hussars on 1 December 1992 to form 'The King's Royal Hussars'.

Terence Cuneo
Terence · Cuneo ·
September 1965

Leaving Buckingham Palace for Trooping the Colour, June 1965.

This colourful ceremony which dates from 1755 is traditionally held each year on the second Saturday in June to honour the Sovereign's official birthday. On that day the colour of one of the five regiments of Foot Guards is 'trooped'. The ritual has its origins in medieval warfare when it was vital that every man could recognise his own flag ('colour') and rally to it in battle. So the practice of showing or 'trooping' the colour along the ranks of assembled soldiers began. Today the 'Colours' are revered as the symbol of a regiment's honour and achievements in battle.

Cuneo's picture is unique in one respect – it depicts the only Trooping at which both the Queen and the Duke of Edinburgh appeared in the uniform of the same regiment. It was Her Majesty's custom, as Colonel-in-Chief of all the regiments in the Household Division, to wear at the parade marking her official birthday the uniform of the particular regiment whose colour was being trooped that year. On the other hand, the Duke of Edinburgh, as Colonel of the Welsh Guards (at that time) would always wear the uniform of that regiment regardless of whose colour was being trooped. In 1965 the regiments were one and the same.

In recent years the Queen has attended the trooping in a small horse-drawn carriage – and has not worn uniform. The Prince of Wales succeeded his father as Colonel of the Welsh Guards.

The Sovereign's Parade, Sandhurst 1965.

The Sovereign's Parade marks the climax of a long period of study and hard training when the cadets who have successfully completed the course pass out from the Royal Military Academy, Sandhurst, to be commissioned as officers in the various corps or regiments of the Army. The best cadet is awarded the Sword of Honour.

Cuneo's picture shows the Commandant of the Royal Military Academy, Major-General John Mogg, in attendance on Her Majesty the Queen. Many years before, he was himself commissioned from Sandhurst into the Oxfordshire and Buckinghamshire Light Infantry. He won the Sword of Honour.

Chinese Ambush. May 1955.

All the studies for this were made in the Malaysian jungle with a detachment of British-trained Malaysian commandos. The trip could hardly be described as dull. Cuneo was taken through a variety of jungle scenery – up and down hills, often in menacingly thick vegetation, through streams and across wobbly rope bridges. Having at last found an ideal spot for the ambush scene, things rapidly came to life. The various poses were adopted with a will – shooting positions, dead bodies, running figures, grenade throwers, etc. Some acting as Chinese, others as Malaysian troops. It all looked extremely realistic, particularly when a 'thunder flash' was loosed off to give the show an added flavour of jungle warfare. The effects of the detonation were amazing. Suddenly, utter silence throughout. The shrill chattering of monkeys, bird calls and the perpetual singing of insects all silenced. Nothing. Not a sound. Then, slowly, very slowly, almost apologetically, one solitary sound from some creature, followed by another, then another and another, until the song of the jungle was in full voice once more. Cuneo enjoyed his jungle trip immensely.

Air Drop, Beria Straits. 1967.

A Shackleton aircraft of the Postal and Courier Service, Royal Engineers, drops a container of mail which will be duly picked up by the carrier's escort.

Cuneo's mouse is always drawn in proportion to the picture. In this case he had to put him well into the foreground. An unenviable situation but a Cuneo mouse always survives!

Withdrawal of an observation post

Temple Cliffs, Aden, 20 June 1967.

"To pull the terribly injured wireless operator from a burning helicopter, return for the pilot and drag him unconscious from the wreck, before calmly radioing for help (all under sniper fire), denotes bravery of a pretty high order. Yet when Northumberland Fusilier Duffy came down to my studio to pose for this grim picture, I could hardly get him to say a thing about the incident. For his gallantry he was awarded the Distinguished Conduct Medal."

RMY
· TERENCE · CUNEO ·
MARCH 1968

Ceremonial Parade

1st Bn Gloucestershire Regiment at Brooke Barracks, Berlin, 1969.

HRH The Duchess of Gloucester and General Ferguson, Commander of the US Army Garrison in Berlin, are shown attaching the Solma-Ri streamer to the Regimental colour. Spandau Prison (now demolished), where Rudolf Hess was imprisoned for over 40 years until his death, can be seen behind the guardroom gate in the centre background.

The history of 'The Gloucesters' goes back some 300 years and three unique achievements typify their glorious record. First, no single regiment bears more battle honours on its Regimental Colour. Second, after the Battle of Alexandria in 1801, which effectively prevented the French invasion of India, the Regiment (then the 28th Foot) was granted the distinction of wearing a badge on the back of the head-dress as well as the front to mark their stout resistance to French attacks launched simultaneously from front and rear. The 'back-badge' is worn to this day. The third distinction is that, alone in the British infantry, it holds the signal honour of the United States Presidential Distinguished Unit Citation for "sustained brilliance in battle, resoluteness and extraordinary heroism". In April 1951 at the River Imjin, near Solma-Ri in Korea, the 1st Battalion, the Gloucestershire Regiment stood firm against a savage and sustained onslaught by the 63rd Communist Chinese Army. After four days they were overwhelmed by vastly superior numbers but every yard of ground they yielded was covered with enemy dead. Their heroic stand bought time for other units of the United Nations force to regroup and block the enemy advance.
In the words of the citation, their conduct in battle "set them apart and above other units participating and reflected unsurpassed credit on these courageous soldiers and their homeland". King George VI gave approval for the emblem of the Presidential Citation (a small oblong of dark blue watered-silk ribbon edged in gold) to be worn at the top of each sleeve of the uniform by all members of the Regiment.

28

The Royal Review, Woolwich, 1969.

This painting, which now hangs in the Sergeants Mess of Headquarters Royal Artillery at Woolwich, shows the Queen as Captain-General reviewing the Royal Regiment. Every type of gun then in the Regiment is on parade, led by the Abbot guns of N Battery – the Eagle Troop – in the foreground.

The Freedom of the City of Nottingham

1st Regiment Royal Horse Artillery, 22 April 1970.

The painting depicts the granting of Civic Honours and Freedom by the City of Nottingham to 1st RHA, who had been recruiting from that area since the War and who had fought throughout the desert battles alongside the South Nottinghamshire Hussars. In the foreground the Mounted Band of the Royal Artillery and four mounted Gunners in full dress lead the parade some two miles through the city. The painting shows the Lord Mayor with the Master Gunner St. James's Park, General Sir Robert Mansergh, taking the salute. E Battery under Major Brian Carr RHA is drawn up outside the Council House, with the Coat of Arms of the City on the gun shields. Colonel Martin Farndale, in the first landrover with RSM Coward, leads his Regiment with the Second-in-Command, Major Brian Moore, and the Adjutant, Captain Gregory Hyland, following. Next comes the Chestnut Troop, under Major David Thatcher, followed by B Battery, whose landrover's nose is just appearing on the extreme right, under Major David Mackintosh.

This treasured painting is with the Regiment who exercise their privileges in Nottingham every ten years or so.

Centenary Commemoration Polo Match

This painting is of the polo match played at Windsor on 28 June 1970, between the 9th/12th Royal Lancers (Prince of Wales's) and the Royal Hussars, to commemorate the centenary of the introduction of polo to England. The original match was played between the 9th Lancers and the 10th Hussars.

This picture was presented to the 9th/12th Lancers by Lieutenant-Colonel Stug Perry who joined the 9th Lancers in 1929 and commanded the Regiment from 1944 to 1946. It shows Colonel Perry hitting a back-hander and, to his left, Prince Philip, The Duke of Edinburgh, who acted as umpire.

TERENCE CUNEO
DECEMBER 1970

Changing the Guard at Buckingham Palace

The Scots Guards hand over to the 7th (DEO) Gurkha Rifles.
24 December, 1971.

This was the first time in their history that Gurkhas had been accorded this honour.

Cuneo recalls: "I sat perched on a table placed up against an open window on the ground floor of Buckingham Palace to paint this picture. It is a little ironic that not one Gurkha was in a position where his kukri showed in my painting. Therefore my mouse was pressed into service to display the famous weapon of that equally famous regiment!"

TERENCE · CUNEO ·
MARCH '72

Portrait of Monty. 1972.

Cuneo recalls a very special occasion:

"One day I received a letter from the Commandant of the Staff College, Camberley in which he expressed concern that among all the portraits at the College there was not a single one of Field Marshal Montgomery. Would I undertake the commission? Would I! After negotiation with Camberley I rang Monty's housekeeper at Isington Mill and asked if I might come down. I was invited to tea that same day and over an enormous slice of cake, told him of the project and its problems. Monty was delighted with the idea and I went away with his promise that I should have his famous double-badged beret, leather jerkin, sweater and field glasses. But the most valuable contribution came from the College in the shape of an officer sent as a possible stand-in for the Field Marshal. This major bore a remarkable resemblance to Monty and although I had to make two more trips to the Mill for additional studies, his help was invaluable. On one such trip, Monty told my wife and me a priceless story which very much reflected his character. On the wall in front of us was a framed photograph of the Victory Parade,1945. Suddenly Monty swung round and stabbed a finger at the line of VIPs in the front row. 'Extraordinary thing, ' he said in his clipped staccato way, 'they're all dying *from the right!* There's Smuts, Churchill, Attlee, Alanbrooke.' He paused, eyeing us fixedly, 'Then we have Alexander and Portal - *neither of them any too fit*!' He left us with impression that the Almighty was in for a fair rap over the knuckles should He decide to interfere with the Field Marshal's plans as to who should still be at the crease when the innings ended.

"The day came when Monty was invited to unveil the finished work, ready hanging in the ante-room of the College. As many of his 'Desert Rats' as could be collected were there for the ceremony. The Field Marshal appeared wearing a blue roll-neck jersey, flannel trousers and slippers. He was in high spirits, beaming on the gathering and chatting to everyone. After a short address, he stepped forward and pulled the cord. The curtains parted and then, for the first time, he saw his portrait - finished.

"He was ecstatic. There is no other word. He simply could not take his eyes from the picture and he must have congratulated me at least a dozen times that day. When the party broke up and we all gathered in the hall to see Monty off, a General turned to me. 'You know, Cuneo, this picture of yours has given the man another year of life'. Somehow, I felt this was true."

Ceremony of the Keys.

The ceremonial locking of the Tower of London has taken place nightly for many centuries. Cuneo has depicted the moment when the Chief Yeoman Warder, the custodian of 'The Queen's Keys', is challenged by the sentry on duty. (In this instance the Tower guard was provided by a Gurkha regiment).

Cuneo recalls: "I may be one of the few people to have had the privilege of having the Tower specially reopened for them after it had been ceremonially locked for the night. The ceremony was reenacted to enable me to follow its progress through the Middle and Byward Towers and on into the yard behind the archway of the sinister Bloody Tower. It was here that I decided to make my picture. By the dim lights of the Tower and the gleam of the carried lantern, the Chief Yeoman Warder, the Watchman and the Guard detail stand frozen in response to the sentry's shouted challenge 'Halt! Who goes there?'. I recall it was a mild night but the Bloody Tower seemed to cast a chill of its own!"

BLOODY TOWER

Leeson Street Patrol

Belfast,February 1973.

Constant patrolling is an essential part of the maintenance of order during internal security operations in Northern Ireland. In his picture 'Tragedy of Ulster' Cuneo has depicted a scene of street violence. Vigorous patrolling aims to prevent such violence erupting.

SP
THE
BAR
FIGHT

E Battery, Royal Horse Artillery

Detmold, Germany. 1974

This picture shows the Battery deploying its 105mm 'Abbot' field guns during exercises near Detmold. The Gun Position Officer, compass in hand, lays out the bearing, while in the background 'Stalwart' amphibious vehicles bring up ammunition. Battery Sergeant Major Blackmore, standing in front of the Gun Position Officer (second from the right), supervises ammunition unloading. On a high rise, Detmold is dominated by a gargantuan but appalling statue known as 'Herman the German' (just visible on the far-distant skyline). This monstrosity, shaped from copper plates, is of truly frightening proportions and, during the war, to show a bit of right thinking, pilots of Spitfires and Hurricans returning from 'ops' used to empty their magazines into Herman.

Whilst Cuneo was working on this painting he was told a nice story by Richard Mountford who commanded the Battery. One day during the war, Goering arrived at Detmold to review the troops and as he strutted down the ranks he caught sight of the statue on the distant skyline. Turning to the commanding officer he demanded "And what is that?" Proudly the CO replied "That, Herr Reichsmarshal, is the statue of our great Herman". Goering coloured slightly. He glanced warmly at the officer and, looking down bashfully, said "Really, you shouldn't have bothered!" It sounds good enough to be true.

E
91 ET 24
CUNEO
DECEMBER
1974

Presentation of Colours

1st, 2nd & 3rd Battalions & the 5th (Volunteer) of The Queen's Regiment. 1974.

Apart from the pageantry, what Cuneo remembers best of this subject is first, having to contend with the dreary background of flats and factories and then, much later, the great pleasure of a trip to Denmark for sittings with Queen Margrethe II and her aide-de-camp. He also recalls the glow he felt when the actual Colours and Drums were brought to his studio – "Still life painting perhaps – but it was like painting history!"

The Master of the Horse.

His Grace, the 10th Duke of Beaufort, KG, PC, GCVO.
(1900-1984).

His Grace succeeded to the Dukedom in 1924 and was Master of the Horse from 1936 to 1978. This portrait was commissioned following subscriptions from some 200 people associated with the Royal Household and the Queen personally presented it to the Duke to mark his 40th anniversary as Master of the Horse. The presentation took place at an evening reception at Buckingham Palace on 11 June 1976 and during that reception Her Majesty drew the artist's attention to an error in the painting. She pointed out that although the Duke's horse, Quebec, had his head drawn well in, the painting showed a long, straight shadow indicative of a horse craning its neck. Cuneo had quite overlooked this detail and so, it seemed, had everyone else. The mistake was quickly rectified.

The 10th Duke was a knowledgeable, experienced and wise Master of the Horse. Had he held office in Queen Victoria's time the story of Her Majesty's first rail journey in 1842 might have ended differently. The following is an extract from James Dugan's *The Great Iron Ship* : "Before the trip the Queen's Master of the Horse went to the station, examined the locomotive according to the Manual of the Horse, and climbed in the cab in his scarlet livery, white gloves and wig. Brunel asked an equerry what this portended. 'The Master of the Horse will, of course, drive the locomotive', he was told. Brunel lured the dutiful courtier to the pilot engine, which ran ahead of the Royal special. The Master of the Horse arrived in London covered in soot and beating away at his wig which was smouldering from sparks. Although the iron horse never succeeded in unsaddling the Master as a court functionary, he has been permanently discouraged from operating Her Majesty's Locomotives."

TERENCE·CUNEO·
JUNE

The Paras have Landed

To achieve the effects Cuneo needed to put this subject over with conviction, he stood on a Surrey heath watching men unload from the sky. That seemingly gentle occupation turned out to be a shade less peaceful than he might have supposed. A container came thumping down missing him by a couple of yards, followed rapidly by a paratrooper, whom he had not spotted, missing him by barely two feet! As the aim was obviously improving, Cuneo decided to move on. Luckily, the grounded figures proved far less menacing to portray.

The Tragedy of Ulster

Northern Ireland, one of the most beautiful parts of the United Kingdom, peopled by kindly men and women of talent and industry, has suffered for years from the activities of a minority committed to the unification of Ireland, north and south, by any methods. Having consistently failed to achieve their airms through the ballot-box they have turned to violence. The IRA (Irish Republican Army), an illegal organisation, uses the tactics of terror, including murder and indicriminate bombing of civilian targets within Ulster and on mainland Britain, to attempt to force the British to abandon the province.

The present period of unrest began in 1969 and the Army was called in to support the Royal Ulster Constabulary in maintaining law and order. Regiments, normally stationed in Germany with Nato, regularly do short emergency tours. The troops are not accompanied by their families, and it is a duty with few attractions.

Cuneo has depicted a scene of street violence. The mob hurls abuse, missiles and petrol bombs at the soldiers who are outnumbered and restricted in their ability to respond. Rioting of this sort has become less prevalent through the increased efficiency of the Police and Army in containing it, but Cuneo's reconstruction typifies the dangerous situation the security forces in Ulster still face every day and which over the years have caused so many violent deaths.

MIST
PHARMACY
PROVO
RULE
OK
ARMY OUT
I R A

The Price of Freedom. 1977.

To be asked to represent the embodiment of the entire British Army in a single painting is a pictorial impossibility. After fruitless attempts at the impossible, Cuneo knew his only hope lay in symbolising the subject, reducing the theme to one simple, dominating figure - the British Soldier. This one figure would somehow have to convey the message. In Lance Sergeant Thompson, Scots Guards, who posed for him, Cuneo felt confident that he had found such a soldier. The painting shown to Her Majesty the Queen at the Review of the Rhine Army in Germany was also the subject of a special philatelic cover commemorating the Review.

The Queen's Birthday Parade

Trooping the Colour. 1st Bn Scots Guards, June 1977.

The artist recalls:

"Although I was able to get some useful drawings of the horsemen of Her Majesty's party, I decided to hire a professional photographer to get me just one shot of the on-coming troops as this, of course, would be quite impossible to sketch in the time at my disposal. Thus, confident of his ability, I went on happily drawing this and that and making various colour notes.

"When the march-past began, I turned to the photographer to warn him that our moment was at hand. To my horror I saw him fiddling with the camera, the lens in his hand. 'What's wrong, for God's sake?' I hissed. 'Can't understand it', he mumbled, 'the shutter seems to have jammed.' 'Haven't you got another camera?' He shook his head and continued to waffle away, while I experienced an overwhelming desire to hammer his top hat into his brain! The parade came on, the Queen lifted her arm in salute and the Colours dipped, and my subject had gone!

"When at last the painting was completed several people of note came to my studio to view it. One of them spotted the mouse, marching proudly behind the Ensign carrying the Guards Colour, dipping his own tiny standard in irreproachable manner. 'Why on earth have you shown your mouse with an RAF standard?' he asked. 'RAF Colours? My dear sir, you really display the most appalling ignorance. Those are certainly not RAF Colours. That is the standard of the Vole-Souris clan. A blue background and a gold circle holding a sliced cheese and the motto *Mort aux Chats* in gold, encompassing it.' I was offered a humble apology - and rightly so!"

TERENCE · CUNEO ·
AUGUST · 1977

B Battery Royal Horse Artillery

with 155-mm guns at Topcliffe, Yorkshire. May 1982.

This painting was commissioned to portray B Battery with their new Field Howitzer 70 when stationed at Topcliffe as part of 1st Regiment RHA. It is a splendid example of precision and accurate painting and shows D Sub-section of the Battery coming into action on the square outside the aircraft hangars of Topcliffe Airfield in May 1982.

Lieutenant-Colonel H. Jones, VC

2nd Bn. Parachute Regiment. The Battle for Goose Green and Darwin, Falkland Islands. 28 May, 1982

At 8 pm on 26 May 1982, 2 Para, carrying 48 hours of arctic rations and an immense load of extra ammunition, moved against Goose Green and Darwin. Wet, cold and tired, they reached Camilla Creek at 3 am and took shelter in some abandoned buildings. 'H', as Colonel Jones was universally known, wanted his men to be as dry and rested as possible before they marched into battle later that night. Meanwhile at 2.35 am 'A' Company, under Major Dair Farrar-Hockley, moved silently forward on to their first objective, quickly silencing the enemy with small-arms and genades. By 5.30 am the second objective had been reached and H moved forward to meet Dair. He ordered the advance to continue but the precious cover of darkness was ebbing away and as dawn broke they came under intense fire from the Argentinians who were waiting for them in strength. The balance of the battle began to slip away from the Paras. They were caught in open ground, outranged by the enemy machine guns and without the artillery support they had hoped for. They seemed powerless to end the bloody deadlock the Argentinians had imposed.

Impatient, H lay beside Farrar-Hockley. "Dair", he said, "You've got to take that ridge." Farrar-Hockley moved forward with some 16 men but three were killed almost at once and he was forced to crawl back whence they had come. A little way back he met Tony Rice, the artillery battery commander. "For God's sake come quickly", he said. "The colonel's gone round the corner on his own." H had pinpointed a machine gun he believed he could take out. Clutching his Sterling sub-machine carbine he dashed fast up a gully towards it. He ran on through heavy fire and seconds later was hit in the neck and fell mortally wounded. Yet even a he lay dying the turning point in A Company's action came. Machine gun and 66 mm rocket fire was silencing the enemy trenches one by one and the first white flags began to appear. Some enemy mortar and artillery fire still came down but the resistance was crumbling. As he knelt beside H, Farrar-Hockley saw his eyelids flicker. He held the colonel's hand until it was obvious he was dead.

2 Para went on to take Goose Green, losing in all 17 killed and 35 wounded; a bitter price but a remarkably small one for a battle of such length and ferocity. The real measure of 2 Para's achievement was that they had prevailed against a well-armed enemy of four times their own strength. The Argentinians had been given a devastating demonstration of Britain's absolute will to achieve victory at whatever cost in blood and treasure.

To all who knew him, the manner of Colonel Jones' death was characteristic. His action was a classically romantic heroic gesture, the deed of a man to whom Goose Green represented the climax of a lifetime as a soldier, and who could not watch his men do that which he would not do himself. H was determined to break the deadlock. His lonely charge was an act in the British Army's great tradition of battalion leadership on the battlefield. This warm, impulsive, utterly dedicated soldier became a national hero with his death and received the posthumous award of the Victoria Cross.

(This was culled from an account in "The Battle for the Falklands" by Max Hastings and Simon Jenkins. Hastings was a war-correspondent with the Task Force and followed every stage from the departure from Portsmouth until he walked alone into Port Stanley, ahead of the British vanguard. Now editor of the *Daily Telegraph*, he generously gave permission for his material to be used).

The Battle of Tumbledown Mountain

The Falkland Islands. 2nd Bn Scots Guards, 14 June 1982.

On 2 April 1982, in spite of clear warnings from Britain not to do so, Argentina invaded the Falkland Islands, a small British dependency in the South Atlantic. The Islands' token defence force, a small detachment of Royal Marines, resisted bravely but was soon overpowered and the Argentine flag was raised. Ignoring Britain's demands that they withdraw, the invaders persisted in their unlawful occupation and Britain was forced into military action to recover the colony. Despite the enormous logistical problems of maintaining it more than 8,000 miles from the United Kingdom base, a Task Force was assembled and set sail for the South Atlantic on 5 and 6 April 1982.

Two months later nearly 1,000 men were dead – including 255 British – and the Falklands had seen the biggest air/sea battles since World War II. The homely names of quiet places – Bluff Cove, Goose Green and Tumbledown Mountain – were to ring round the world for the saddest of reasons; they had become arenas of bitter conflict, bloodshed and death. The many awards for bravery, amongst them two posthumous Victoria Crosses, bore witness to the price of restoring the territory to the Falkland Islanders.

Cuneo has depicted the savage encounter on 14 June 1982 when the Scots Guards captured one of the most strongly defended positions of the entire campaign. Their casualties were nine killed and 43 wounded. Tumbledown Mountain was the decisive battle in the action to recover the Falklands. Before the day was out all the Argentine Forces had surrendered.

Lull in the Battle

The Army Catering Corps with 3 Para at Port San Carlos, Falkland Islands, May 1982.

Time was when regimental cooks were figures of fun, the butt of ribald humour, whose culinary adventures with tin-opener and frying-pan were anticipated more with anxiety than pleasure. If heard at all, the words 'Bon appetit' were spoken only in jest. Into this gastronomic wasteland rode the Army Catering Corps to work an almost magical transformation on Army food. Varied, satisfying and imaginative menus became the norm and for the first time the soldier was offered several choices where formerly he had only one – take it or leave it. The ACC established and maintains superb professional standards. They knew they were good and proved it by competing with civilian chefs from London and Paris in international contests – and beating them. Today the quality of catering in the Army is widely acclaimed as being of the highest class.

Although catering is its prime function, the ACC takes on many extra tasks on active service. Cuneo's picture is a composite of the jobs they did during the Falklands action – stretcher bearers and medical assistants, helicopter marshalling and loading, manning weapons pits, storage of weapons and ammunition, watchkeeping and guarding prisoners of war – and still having the evening meal ready on time.

MUNRO
SEPTEMBER 1984

‘Outrage’

Hyde Park, London. July 1982.

Cuneo became very involved emotionally in this work. It shows Sefton, a 19-year old cavalry horse, bearing the scars of an IRA bomb that on 20 July 1982 killed four members of the Blues and Royals and maimed seven other horses so badly that they had to be shot. The preliminary sketches were done little more than 24 hours after this obscene act of cruelty was perpetrated. In a remarkable way, Sefton became the focus for thousands of ordinary people throughout the world to express sympathy for all who had suffered that day. Sefton, by his dignity in great pain and brave determination to recover became a symbol that, in the end, good will triumph over evil. The full story is on page 25. Sefton made a full recovery and retired to the Home of Rest for Horses at Speen Farm in Buckinghamshire where he enjoyed the loving care and attention he so bravely earned, until he died on 9 July 1993 at the age of thirty.

CUNEO
AUGUST 1982

His Majesty, King Hussein of Jordan, painted in the Palace, in Amman, 1980.

Field Marshal Sherif Zeid Ben Shaker, Commander-in-Chief, Jordanian Armed Forces

The Queen's visit to the Staff College Camberley. 1982.

It is usual for a number of students from Foreign and Commonwealth countries to attend the staff course at Camberley. This painting shows the Queen visiting the Overseas Students' Exhibition in the Alanbrooke Hall. Her Majesty is talking to the Pakistani student and his family.

Exercise Lionheart. Hanover, Germany. 1984.

In this painting commissioned by HQ 1st (British) Corps, Cuneo was expected to achieve the impossible – to portray a major British exercise in Germany in the 1980s on a single canvas. The exercise was held in the Hanover area of Germany in September 1984.

The picture shows a bridge that the sappers have just put across the river; their combat engineer tractor (with a bucket) is over the river on the left of the scene. A troop (three) of Challenger tanks are over the bridge and moving on to engage 'enemy' in the black smoke in the distance. An artillery observer is coming on to the bridge on the extreme left. Infantry are already over in the bushes and in the distance more Challengers and Warrior armoured personnel carriers are moving off to attack. Beside the bridge sits a self-propelled Rapier air-defence missile detachment. Overhead, RAF Harriers attack the 'enemy' position; Lynx anti-tank and a Gazelle helicopter of the Army Air Corps move up in support. Medics of the Royal Army Medical Corps, in gas masks, attend to a casualty. A pallet of ammunition, provided by the Ordnance Corps can be seen by the bridge.

But this is an exercise and not a real 'action' – hence the coloured smoke, to simulate battle, and the group of umpires by the bridge, wearing white arm-bands. If you look closely there is an armoured personnel carrier just beyond the engineer tractor (a '432' in the jargon) with a white cross on its side, to indicate that it is also an umpire.

The detail in this picture is quite superb. 'Lionheart' turned out to be the last big exercise of the 'Cold War'.

This cartoon was presented by the artist to Martin Farndale (the Corps Commander) after the exercise. It depicts much of the same scenario as the actual painting but Cuneo has superimposed himself in a helicopter careering over the 'battle' area. Below, can be seen in the centre General Sir Martin Farndale trying to placate his staff about his eccentric artist friend leaning out of the helicopter. On the right, is Brigadier Charles Guthrie, the Chief of Staff, later to command 1st (British) Corps himself, and on the left is Lieutenant-Colonel Hugh Pike, later to command the 3rd Division.

This cartoon brings back many happy memories to all concerned who grew to like, respect and admire their eccentric artist who showed such supreme skill in capturing their exercise for all time on one splendid canvas.

The painting still hangs in the Mess of the Corps, now the ACE Rapid Reaction Corps, composed of regiments from many NATO armies.

'Coming Home'. Painted in 1986.

An illustration to a novel by Alan North commissioned by the author. A damaged Lancaster bomber is hidden by the French at St Amour and the day the renovation is complete, the entire village turns out to drag their prize onto a makeshift runway for take off.

CUNEO
FEBRUARY 1987

The Search. The Ulster Defence Regiment, 1986.

Two French rifles and a sawn-off shot gun were found hidden beneath straw in a manger in this half-ruined old barn in County Tyrone. Cuneo went on several patrols with the regiment through the most lovely Irish countryside - "I found it hard to believe that here, alongside the good and peaceful ways of life, skulked the murderers with their threat of mutilation and death. The stark tragedy of it all."

Cuneo
June '86

First Light, March 1990.

American heavy tanks on exercise in Germany. "It wasn't only a mud bath for the tanks, but I was dry occasionally and anyway they were a grand crowd to work with. A slippery but enjoyable trip."

CUNEO
MARCH 1990

Operation Desert Storm, 1991.

In late 1990 President Saddam Hussein of Iraq invaded Kuwait. Despite continuous diplomatic pressure and imposition of sanctions by the United Nations, he refused to withdraw, announcing that he had annexed the territory. Finally, all other measures having failed, the UN authorised military action to clear the invaders from Kuwait.
A combined land, sea and air force under the overall command of General H. Norman Schwarzkopf ('Stormin' Norman'), US Army was despatched. The United States was the major contributor to the UN action and was supported by Britain and other nations. The senior British Army Commander was Lt. General Sir Peter de la Billiere and the British force included the 7th Armoured Brigade (Desert Rats) and the 4th Armoured Brigade. The Royal Air Force led the early attacks on Iraqi military targets with great success. The land battle when it came was brief and equally successful. Kuwait was cleared of all invaders.

At the instigation of Lord Rothermere of the Daily Mail, two paintings were commissioned to commemorate British participation in the Gulf War. One, by Frank Wootton, showing RAF aircraft taking off for a strike on Iraqi targets; and the other by Terence Cuneo. Cuneo's painting was based on sketches made on the tank training ground at Bovington and captures the atmosphere of the brief but fierce battle in which 7th and 4th Armoured Brigades played a vital part.

The Duke of Kent formally accepted both paintings from Lord Rothermere on 13th December 1991. It was announced that both would be sold in aid of the Army and RAF Benevolent Funds. A limited edition of fine art prints of these paintings went on sale at the same time.

General Sir Peter de la Billiere signing prints of 'Desert Storm'.

CUNEO
JULY 1991

The Basrah Road

The Queen's Royal Irish Hussars.
Closing stages of the Gulf War. G+4 - 28 February 1991.

An hour after midnight the Queen's Royal Irish Hussars were informed by their Brigade Headquarters that a temporary cease-fire had been agreed, starting at 0500 hours local time. The Regiment was to hold tight in their current positions, 50 kilometres due west of Kuwait City. Four hours later came the information that there had been a misunderstanding over the time difference between the United States and the Middle East and the cease fire was to be deferred until 08.00 hours. The Regiment was ordered to move to the Basrah road at best speed to cut off the withdrawal of the Iraqis from Kuwait City.

They moved at about 0620 hours. The weather was overcast and the dense smog from the oil fires to the south blackened the sky, reducing visibility in some areas to less than 400 metres. To minimise the risk of being fired on in such conditions by friendly forces, orders were given that the Regiment should fly whatever flags they had to assist identification .

At 07.50 hours, having covered the distance at remarkable speed, the Regiment reached the Basrah road and took up defensive positions. Evidence of the Iraqis' hurried flight was everywhere; abandoned vehicles, discarded materiel of every sort, and dead bodies. It was a grim sight. At 08.00 hours Martin Bell, the BBC reporter travelling with the Regiment announced that the cease fire was in force.

Cuneo's painting shows the Regimental HQ of the Queen's Royal Irish Hussars as they set up at 08.00 hours after the morning's rapid move to the Basrah road. Lt. Col. Arthur Denaro is standing on his tank, "Churchill" with his second-in-command, Mark O'Reilly, and the operations officer, Robert Hutton, leaning on the front of the tank.

This painting is a good example of Cuneo's rare talent for depicting an incident in battle, based on accounts given by those who took part. The event was entirely 're-staged' in Germany since the Regiment had brought all its armour back from the Gulf before the artist was commissioned to paint the picture for the Officers' Mess. Cuneo has shown the final tense moments in the Gulf War when the Regiment, their Colours and Jacks fluttering from aerial masts, waited on the Basrah road in the wind-swept gloom for news that the war was finally over.

When the painting was delivered to the Regiment at Fallingbostel in Germany, Arthur Denaro wrote to Cuneo:

"It is exactly what we all wanted and more: its appeal has stretched so far beyond the Officers' Mess that I have decided it should be a regimental picture and hang in Regimental Headquarters. It captures that moment, 8 a.m. on 28th February, so well: the atmosphere, the gloom, the wind and the power. There is also in it that great sense of relief that we all felt."

Nothing could have pleased Cuneo more than this.

CUNEO
OCTOBER '91

Closing with the Enemy

The Staffordshire Regiment, Iraq. February 1991.

The picture, commissioned by the Sergeants' Mess, shows 1st Bn The Staffordshire Regiment (The Prince of Wales's), 38th, 64th, leading the advance of the 1st (UK) Armoured Division through Iraq, attacking a divisional headquarters with small arms and bayonets fixed.

At 10.00 hours on 25 February 1991, the Regiment crossed the start line leading the main advance into Iraq which was to result in the liberation of Kuwait. In less than 100 hours the Battalion crossed 300 kilometres of desert, capturing seven divisional-sized objectives and taking over 1,500 prisoners of war for the loss of two soldiers killed and five wounded. In recognition of its meritorious service in the Gulf, the Regiment was awarded one OBE, two MCs, five mentions in dispatches, five BEMs and three commendations.

Painted April 1992.

Cuneo
April 1992

The Army Catering Corps in the Gulf. 1991.

During the Gulf War some 850 members of the ACC provided a 24-hour meals service using the No. 4 and No. 5 Field Catering Cooksets. The number of meals provided was greatly in excess of what had originally been planned and, as usual, while coping with the cooking the ACC found time for their many other sundry duties. If ever time hung heavily, there were always Nuclear, Biological and Chemical Warfare drills to be practised.

After the arrival of 1st Division, a 15-man unit cooked for 2,000-3,000 men around the clock. A containerised bakery produced 16,000 rolls a day. It was reported that by early February the Army had consumed three million eggs and 1,200 tons of potatoes – suggesting it may be some time before nouvelle cuisine supplants egg and chips as the soldier's dish of the day.

Cuneo's painting depicts an actual field kitchen, located in a Concentration Area on the Saudi-Iraq border between Hafar al Batin and Al Qaysumah, serving meals to troops of 7th Armoured Brigade (The Desert Rats) before they moved to their pre-attack positions. The No. 4 (trailer-mounted) cookset and the No. 5 (free-standing) cookset are both shown. In this location, over a period of five days, more than 10,000 Allied troops were fed.

CUNEO

Glossary of paintings

Index (Bold figures=illustrations)